CHEAP BASTARD'S® SERIES

THE CHEAP BASTARD'S® GUIDE TO

Portland, Oregon

Secrets of Living the Good Life—**For Less!**

First Edition

Rachel **Dresbeck**

gpp®
travel

Guilford, Connecticut
An imprint of Globe Pequot Press

All the information in this guidebook is subject to change. We recommend that you call ahead to obtain current information before traveling.

To buy books in quantity for corporate use
or incentives, call **(800) 962–0973**
or e-mail **premiums@GlobePequot.com.**

Text design by Sheryl P. Kober
All photos licensed by Shutterstock.com
Map by Daniel Lloyd © Morris Book Publishing, LLC

ISBN 978-0-7627-7302-2

Printed in the United States of America
10 9 8 7 6 5 4 3 2 1

This book is for Flannery and Cleo,
who make this book both possible and necessary.

CONTENTS

Introduction xi

SECTION 1: Entertainment in Portland

Theater: In on the Act 2
    Usher Yourself In .3
    Always Free 7
    Cheap Seats 7
    Youth & Children's Theater 11
    Theater Festivals 12
    Discount Tickets 14

Film: Cheap Shots 15
    Independent Theaters 16
    Alternative Theaters 23
    Free Movies 23
    Film Events 26

Dance: Cheap Moves 27
    Performance 28
    Dance Instruction 31

Music: Of Thee I Sing 33
    Keeping Up: Local Music News 34
    Favorite Venues 35
    Classically Cheap 39
    Community Music 41
    Festivals & Concert Series 43

Readings & Open Mics: Free Expression 46
    Regular Events 47
    Readings at Bookstores 50
    Cheap Readings 53
    Grab the Mic 55

SECTION 2: Living in Portland

Food: Cheap Eats 57

   Happy Hours 58

   Food Carts 64

   Free Samples 68

   Cheap Food. 70

Drinks: Cheap Buzz 78

   Wine Tastings 79

   Beer Tastings. 83

   Beer Festivals 85

   Brewery Tours 88

   Distillery Tours 88

Transportation: On the Road Again 90

   Public Transportation 91

   Car Sharing 93

   Walking 95

   Biking 96

   Biking Resources 97

   Bike Repair. 99

   Heading Out of Town 100

Child's Play: Cheap Activities 102

   Great Playgrounds, Parks & Walks 103

   Farms & Fairs. 105

   Arcade Games 108

   Skateboarding 109

   Story Times 110

   Museums & Attractions 112

Shopping: Bargain Basement 117

   Trash or Treasure 118

   Cheap Fashion 120

   Consignment & Thrift Stores. 124

   Gear on the Cheap 128

Discount Shops & Outlets 129

Do-It-Yourself 131

Health & Medical: An Apple a Day 134

Health Clinics 135

Alternative Health Care 136

Sexual Health 137

Outdoor Recreation, Sports & Fitness: Cheap Thrills 139

Cheap & Free Resources 140

Golf 140

Ski Areas 144

Cross-Country Skiing & Snowshoeing 147

Swimming 148

Tennis 149

Yoga 150

Nosebleed Seats: Spectator Sports 151

Beauty Services: Cheap Is in the Eye of the Beholder 153

Beauty School Drop-In 154

Cheap Barbers & Salons 157

Cheap Relaxation 158

Soaking & Saunas 159

Apartments & Accommodations 161

Free Rental Services 162

Cheap Sleep 163

House-Sitting 164

SECTION 3: Exploring Portland

Walking Tours: A Cents of Place 166

Nature Walks 167

Guided Tours 170

Free Self-Guided Nature Walks 171

Free Self-Guided City Walks 172

Free Gallery Walks 174

Gardens & Forests: Free Range 176

   Free Gardens 177

   Sometimes Free Gardens. 179

   Gardening Resources 181

   Foraging 182

Museums, Public Art & Libraries: Free Access 186

   Free 187

   Sometimes Free. 191

   Cheap 192

   Art Resources 196

Escaping the City: Free at Last 197

   Camping in Oregon 198

   Day Hikes, Swimming Holes & Waterfalls 201

   Hot Springs 207

Appendix A: Additional Resources 209

Appendix B: Parks & Recreation Community Centers 213

Appendix C: Library Locations 216

Index 219

ABOUT THE AUTHOR

Rachel Dresbeck is a writer and editor and the author of the *Insiders' Guide to Portland*, as well as *Oregon Disasters* and the first edition of the *Insiders' Guide to the Oregon Coast*. When she is not researching and writing about ways to be frugal and still have fun, she teaches science writing and writes about research for Oregon Health & Science University. She has lived for nearly twenty years in Portland, one of the best cities in which to live well for much, much less as the best revenge. Join the conversation at http://chezportland.tumblr.com.

ACKNOWLEDGMENTS

Living well while being frugal is simply not possible without a strong community—without them, this book and many other things would not be possible. I would like to thank my bargain-minded friends who have made thrifting fun. Especially, my thanks to Cara Bolles, who has shared many adventures in and conversations about frugality over the years. Thanks also to Linda Colwell, Nancy Forrest, John Grochau, and Kerry Kelvin, who are my guides to the feasting part of the feast of life that is Portland, Oregon. In the years that I have lived in and written about Portland, I have met a multitude of experts who are willing to share their knowledge and enthusiasm for free because they just love this city so much, and I am truly in their debt. When I asked my daughter who should go in the acknowledgments, she said, "Portland, because it's such a beautiful city and it's so easy to live here." I agree! Thanks, Portland!

A big shout-out is also due to my wonderful neighbors, who helped out with their amazing support, including bringing me chocolate, driving my daughters places, and feeding them dinner, half the time without my knowing (Me: I need to stop writing to make you dinner. Them: We ate at Chris's already). Thanks especially to Chris Frost, who is the inspiration for many of these bargains, to Ann Marcus, to Steve and Patty Banchero, and to Kayleen Shiba for partially adopting my younger daughter in these past weeks.

When my editor at Globe Pequot, Kevin Sirois, offered me the chance to write this book, I was thrilled, since I figured I had in fact already written this book. At least in my head. It turns out that it was not quite as simple, so thank you to Kevin Sirois for being a great and patient editor—and to the rest of the thoughtful editing team at Globe Pequot.

Finally, thanks are especially due to my darling, neglected family—my husband Tom and my daughters Flannery and Cleo, and our long-suffering, tennis-ball-game-deprived dog, Lily. Without your encouragement, I couldn't do anything I do.

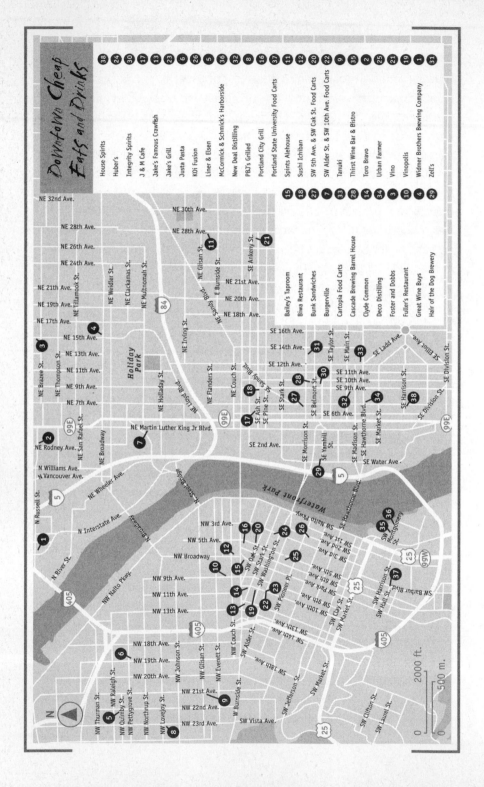

Downtown Cheap Eats and Drinks

38 House Spirits
24 Huber's
30 Integrity Spirits
17 J & M Cafe
13 Jake's Famous Crawfish
23 Jake's Grill
6 Justa Pasta
26 KOi Fusion
5 Liner & Elsen
36 McCormick & Schmick's Harborside
32 New Deal Distilling
8 PBJ's Grilled
16 Portland City Grill
37 Portland State University Food Carts
11 Spints Alehouse
12 Sushi Ichiban
20 SW 5th Ave. & SW Oak St. Food Carts
22 SW Alder St. & SW 10th Ave. Food Carts
9 Tanuki
35 Thirst Wine Bar & Bistro
2 Toro Bravo
25 Urban Farmer
21 Vino
19 Vinopolis
1 Widmer Brothers Brewing Company
31 Zell's

15 Bailey's Taproom
18 Biwa Restaurant
27 Bunk Sandwiches
7 Burgerville
33 Cartopia Food Carts
28 Cascade Brewing Barrel House
14 Clyde Common
34 Deco Distilling
3 Foster and Dobbs
10 Fuller's Restaurant
4 Great Wine Buys
29 Hair of the Dog Brewery

INTRODUCTION

I have not always been a cheap bastard. Oh, I had my moments. As an impoverished student, when I had to live cheaply out of necessity, I learned to be chic while shopping entirely at Goodwill. After college, living in an expensive city in my first job, I learned to throw elegant dinner parties for 12 using four lemons and a pound of pasta from Trader Joe's. I bought furniture at yard sales, rode the bus, swapped clothing, did extra freelance work, and still managed to have fun. But the goal was always to get a job where I could pay full price without blinking—to stop being cheap. And I did just that, happily relinquishing my cheap ways, with my family equally happy to go along. When movements such as the Compact—where you abstain from purchasing anything new for a year—arrived on the scene, we were not impressed. We had been there already, and we knew if we had to live like cheap bastards, we could.

Eventually, however, my children expressed the desire to attend an institution of higher education. By then, we were used to lavish dinners out, travel abroad, nice cars, summer camps, lessons, and other accoutrements of modern American family life. Though we had started to save for college, rising costs were outstripping the original savings plan, and our aversion to debt led us to one conclusion: We must return to our frugal ways.

But something was different this time. For one thing, it wasn't just me. There now is an army out there of the newly frugal. Many are forced by circumstance, while others embrace frugality voluntarily. But regardless of the reason, we are cultivating the habits of our grandparents. All this shared experience of hunting down sweet deals demands lively conversation.

Not all bargains are created equal, however. Just because something is "free" doesn't mean it's worth having. A classic example is found in the affectionate IFC (Independent Film Channel) parody of Portland life *Portlandia* (tag line: "Portland: The city where young people go to retire"). One episode features a couple of dumpster-diving hipsters who not only dig furniture, clothing, and small koala bears out of the trash, but also expired food. Expired food that they use to throw a dinner party, in one of the more revolting scenes in televised sketch comedy. The term "cheap bastard" thus requires some clarification; I mean "cheap bastard" lightly—I mean it in the sense of frugality and value—quality over quantity, maximum experience over the dopamine rush of getting something for nothing. Revolting, expired-food dinner parties are not the purpose of this book. Instead, the purpose of this book is not only to help you learn how to live cheaply in the beautiful city of Portland, Oregon, but also to live well.

Here you will find a range of free, almost free, and cheap things to do, eat, wear, have, and get around with, from the more obvious to the more obscure, concentrating especially on what Portland is known for. *New York Times* writer Matt Gross, the Frugal Traveler, fell in love with Portland's quality-of-life sensibility, writing, "Amid economic catastrophe—Oregon has the country's second-highest unemployment rate—there was a general indifference to wealth. In its place was a dedication to the things that really matter: hearty food and drink, cultural pursuits both high and low, days in the outdoors and evenings out with friends. It's the good life, and in Portland it still comes cheap." This is an astute observation. The guiding principle driving this book is *quality* for cheap or free—especially food, drink, and the basics of a well-lived daily life. That is, this book agrees with the poet George Herbert: "Living well is the best revenge."

A few notes on how this book is organized. Essentially, you'll find three categories: free, free but with a caveat, and really cheap. There are sometimes caveats that come with cheap and free things—well, there always are in some ways—an investment of time, a minimum drink purchase, less-than-ideal viewing conditions, for example. When these are formal requirements, then I've noted the listing with *The Catch.*

Everything here points toward participating in the adventure of life, in ways that are not only morally sound but also legal: You won't find unethical gimmicks or cheating. And while I am a fan of bartering and bargaining, at least in theory, nothing in this book leads you down that path.

One thing that I have learned from writing books like this is that things change rapidly and without warning. Many businesses close, open, change their menus, change their hours, stop offering specials—or start offering them. While I have done my best to catalog as many free and cheap options as possible, and they should be accurate at press time, it's wise to be prepared. Check to make sure that free event is still free before you show up; call ahead or look up the listing online.

Finally, you should consider this guide as a starting point. New free things and bargains are created every day to delight the hearts of the cheap. Take this book as a road map for creating your own adventure.

Entertainment in Portland

THEATER:
IN ON THE ACT

"I have the terrible feeling that, because I am wearing a white beard and am sitting in the back of the theatre, you expect me to tell you the truth about something. These are the cheap seats, not Mount Sinai."

—ORSON WELLES

While it's not New York—or even Seattle—Portland still has a lot going for it in the theater department. We have a number of playhouses, performers, and production companies with national reputations. And Portland's DIY spirit is alive and well in its theater community, so you will find many new works from local playwrights being staged for the first time, in addition to a healthy menu of classical productions.

That said, Portland's theater scene is scaled for Portland. Thus, while in many cities, becoming a volunteer usher is the ideal way to feed your theater-going habit for free, in Portland, not so much. It's not that there are no opportunities, but so many of the theater companies are low-budget enough that they do all the volunteer work themselves—training and maintaining a volunteer corps requires a staff member and a lot of effort. So it's worth it for the bigger companies, but not for the smaller ones. And some of the opportunities that exist are for discounted tickets rather than free shows. But that is not to say there are no opportunities. Here are the performance venues and theater companies that could use your help.

USHER **YOURSELF** IN

Artists Repertory Theater
1515 SW Morrison St.
(503) 241-1278
www.artistsrep.org

The Catch: Ushers can see the show for free, but parking costs you $5.

This company has 2 beautiful, spare, black-box theaters in which they perform contemporary and classic plays, including West Coast and national premieres. They make heavy use of volunteer ushers, especially physically fit ones that can help patrons up and down the stairs. Ushers can see the show for which they are volunteering, unless it's sold out—in which case, you will receive 2 free tickets to a different performance. There is a waiting list for ushers, and you'll need to read their extensive usher guide and fill out an application. For cheap seats, show up 1 hour before the show: Rush tickets are $20 (and subject, of course, to availability). Students with ID can see shows for $20.

Broadway Rose New Stage Theatre

12850 SW Grant Ave., Tigard
(503) 620-5262
www.broadwayrose.org

Summer performances:
Deb Fennell Auditorium
9000 SW Durham Rd.

This professional company—the largest professional musical company in the state—offers 6 main-stage Broadway musicals, comedies, and similar shows annually, along with children's theater. They rely on volunteers for many performance-related tasks, including ticket-taking, selling tickets and concessions, and ushering. If musicals are your thing, this is a great opportunity, since ushers do get to see the show. To find out about volunteering, contact Emma Lubin, the volunteer coordinator, at (503) 906-2378 or via the website.

Lakewood Center for the Arts

368 S. State St., Lake Oswego
(503) 635-3901
www.lakewood-center.org

This pretty playhouse in suburban Lake Oswego stages excellent productions of classic and modern plays, and they utilize volunteers for office work, set work, fund-raising, and ushering. If you are interested in ushering, call the number listed above.

Miracle Theater

425 SE 6th Ave.
(503) 236-7253
www.milagro.org

This popular arts and cultural organization presents English-language and bilingual plays and performances by Hispanic playwrights. Often their productions are world premieres; many are by local writers—but old or new, they are always inventive and challenging. They use volunteers in many capacities and have a handy online form if you want to indicate your interest.

Portland Center for the Performing Arts

1111 SW Broadway
(503) 274-6566
www.pcpa.com

This is Portland's largest and fanciest performance space—or actually three spaces: **Antoinette Hatfield Hall** (which holds the Dolores Winningstad Theatre, Newmark Theatre, and Brunish Hall); **Arlene Schnitzer Concert Hall;** and **Keller Auditorium.** With almost 1,000 performances of every variety per year, from lectures to Warren Miller movies to touring productions of musicals such as *Wicked* to the Oregon Symphony and the Portland Opera, there is plenty of work for volunteers to do. (Interestingly, theater is a relatively small proportion of these performances.) Volunteers undergo rigorous training for their many jobs, which can include office work and giving tours as well as ushering. Ushers are used primarily by the Newmark and Winningstad Theatres; they perform the usual duties of showing people to their seats, as well as taking tickets and handing out programs. Greeters are used at the Keller Auditorium and the Arlene Schnitzer Concert Hall—these are the prized volunteer spots, since the most exciting national acts use these forums. You're eligible to become a greeter after numerous tours of duty at the Newmark and Winningstad. To enlist as a volunteer usher, you'll need to download and fill out an application form from the website (look under the tab that says "Information") and be prepared to be put on the waiting list. Since this vast venue is not home to one particular company, your best bet for cheap tickets is either Goldstar.com or checking with the group that's actually performing to see if rush or other discounts are available.

Portland Center Stage

Gerding Theater
128 NW 11th Ave.
(503) 445-3700
www.pcs.org

Portland Center Stage is the city's largest Equity house, producing new works, classics, musicals, and every other theatrical genre. You will see tried and true audience favorites as well as world premieres, all under the expert guidance of artistic director Chris Coleman. The winter holiday season is especially popular, with beloved productions such as *A Christmas Carol* and

The Santaland Diaries counted as traditions among many Portland households. This busy theater relies on volunteers not only for ushering but also for newsletters, leading tours, feeding the performers and technical crew, and in other capacities. As an usher, you might see the show, but you might be standing up for the duration. Volunteers fill out an application downloaded from the website (scroll all the way down to the website footer and click on "Volunteer"), but contact them first to see what the availability is for volunteer usher spots. If you are interested, call the lead house manager at (503) 445-3825 to be added to the list (after you've sent in your application). For cheap seats without volunteering, rush tickets are available 1 hour before performance for $20.

Portland Opera
Keller Auditorium
222 SW Clay St.
(503) 248-4335 (Auditorium)
(503) 241-1802 (Portland Opera)
www.portlandopera.org

The Portland Opera has a national reputation for innovation, since it was an early adopter of supertitles for its performances—and they were the first opera company in the world to sponsor national tours of Broadway musicals. The "Best of Broadway" series not only has helped the Portland Opera remain viable, but it has also brought fantastic productions of popular shows to town, shows such as *Wicked, Les Miserables,* and *Billy Elliot,* for starters. They use volunteers for the opera in a variety of really fun ways—for example, they use production volunteers in non-speaking, non-singing roles (you have to be available for all the rehearsals and performances, of course); as stand-ins for lighting design; and as costumers. They also need volunteers for the usual kinds of things, such as patron events and office work. Benefits include discounted tickets and free dress rehearsal viewings. Greeter and usher roles are organized through Portland Center for the Performing Arts. Rush opera tickets are sold to students, seniors, and military personnel (all with ID) for $10 and for $20 for everyone else; one ticket per person please.

ALWAYS **FREE**

Shakespeare in the Park—Portland Actors Ensemble
www.portlandactors.com

Since the summer of 1970, the Portland Actors Ensemble has been staging Shakespeare plays in city parks entirely for free. This fantastic program puts on at least 6 performances per play each summer, rotating the "stage" from park to park to extend their reach. These are good productions to introduce children to Shakespeare; if you sit at the periphery they can "act" too, and you won't disturb your fellow play-goers. (You won't be able to hear as well, either). Seeing a performance in a park is a very pleasant way to spend a summer afternoon in the city. PAE also holds fund-raisers and other events throughout the year—indoors—to support its free-theater mission.

CHEAP **SEATS**

Beaverton Civic Theatre
Beaverton City Library Auditorium
12375 SW 5th St., Beaverton
(503) 754-9866
www.beavertoncivictheatre.org

Beaverton Civic Theatre is community theater at its best; they perform popular dramas and comedies, as well as offering acting and other workshops—all with an army of 200 volunteers. Tickets are $15 for adults, $12 for seniors and students, and $5 for children 10 and under—but the best deal is on the opening Friday, when you can get a ticket for $5 if you bring a book, CD, or DVD to donate to the library. Parking is free too.

Brody Theater
16 NW Broadway
(503) 224-2227
www.brodytheater.com

The Brody Theater is an improv school that gives its students plenty of stage time to practice. On Wednesday at 9:30 p.m., they host an open mic for $3—here you can watch seasoned professionals as well as comic actors in training. Less cheap shows are also available throughout the week.

CoHo Theater
2257 NW Raleigh St.
(503) 220-2646
www.cohoproductions.org

CoHo is a small production company that collaborates with other companies to produce new works and old in their handsome space in Northwest Portland. Many of their productions are by local playwrights and therefore they offer some groundbreaking theater. Tickets run about $25, but usually they'll have a designated pay-what-you-will performance one night each week. This group lets other companies and performers use its facilities as well, so there is often something interesting happening in the space.

Compass Repertory Theatre
Interstate Firehouse Cultural Center
5340 N. Interstate Ave.
(503) 823-4322
http://compassrep.org

This ensemble infuses new life into theater classics with sharp productions of works such as *'Tis a Pity She's a Whore* and *The Cherry Orchard*. They perform at the Interstate Firehouse Cultural Center in North Portland. Cheap seats include Thursday night specials for $10 per ticket.

Portland Playhouse
602 NE Prescott St.
(503) 205-0715
www.portlandplayhouse.org

The productions by Portland Playhouse range from contemporary classics by Tony Kushner and August Wilson to edgy performances of works by Portland playwrights. They release rush tickets 30 minutes prior to show time. With these, you can't sit down until just before curtain, but on the other hand, you'll pay only $15 to $20 per ticket depending on the seat. Another bonus: Free street parking is available.

Portland Story Theater

Hipbone Gallery
1847 E. Burnside
(503) 231-3994
http://portlandstorytheater.com

Portland Story Theater specializes in narrative arts and spoken-word theater woven together in unconventional ways. These are intimate performances of original works, and they ultimately require a high level of engagement with the audience. They regularly sell out their shows—but if you are lucky, you can get the cheapest tickets for $15.

Profile Theatre

3430 SE Belmont St.
(503) 242-0080
http://profiletheatre.org

Attending Profile Theatre is kind of like taking a special seminar on the works of one playwright: Each season, they devote their productions to staging as many works as they can from one writer. These include staged readings and one-night performances as well as full productions; playwrights featured include contemporary writers as well as modern greats. Only three theaters in the nation organize their seasons this way, and Profile is the only one in the west. You can get discounted tickets on Wednesday night, when performances are $16 ($12 for students).

Readers Theatre Repertory

Blackfish Gallery
420 NW 9th Ave.
www.readerstheatrerep.org

Readers Theatre Repertory performs unconventional productions drawn from the highly neglected one-act literature. When was the last time you saw a one-act? College? High school? These artists found this appalling as well, and hence started RTR. These shows are a good way to acquaint younger audiences with the theater—the shows are not really long, and they choose interesting plays. They perform at the Blackfish Gallery in the Pearl District, making for an intimate theater experience, and while they don't have rush tickets or other deals, the ticket price is designed to be affordable at $8.

Stumptown Stages
Interstate Firehouse Cultural Center
5340 N. Interstate Ave.
(503) 381-8686
www.stumptownstages.com

Stumptown Stages produces musical theater, with works as diverse as *Urinetown* and *Godspell*—as well as original productions. Their primary venue is the Interstate Firehouse Cultural Center, but they also have shows in other local venues. Tickets are not cheap; your best bet is Goldstar.com or the Chinook Book (see below).

Third Rail Repertory Theatre
World Trade Center Theatre
121 SW Salmon
(503) 546-6558
www.thirdrailrep.org

Third Rail is a professional, permanent ensemble company modeled after groups such as Steppenwolf Theater in Chicago—that is, they rely on the synergies of the group to raise the level of the performance. This talented company, which includes Broadway veterans as well as graduates of local theater programs, performs mostly contemporary work. Twenty rush seats for $20 are released 1 hour before show time. They also offer student ($17 off!) and senior ($4 off) discounts, and a 2-for-1 coupon in the Chinook Book. Finally, you can see pay-what-you-will performances on the Thursday prior to opening night and free staged readings of plays the group is exploring.

Twilight Repertory Theater
ShoeBox Theatre
2110 SE 10th Ave.
www.twilightrep.org

The tight ensemble group Twilight Rep produces 3 plays each year, alternating between comedy and drama. You will find everything from Shakespeare to Molière to Albee to Oregon-native David Gallic. Sundays have pay-what-you-will performances; otherwise tickets are $10 to $15.

YOUTH & **CHILDREN'S** THEATER

Blue Monkey Theater Company
Various locations
www.bluemonkeytheater.org

The Catch: If you buy tickets online, there's a $3 fee, but this fee is not waived if you purchase tickets at the box office.

Blue Monkey is a young-adult-focused group producing works that are both challenging and accessible for teen audiences. They do a lot of work with audiences that typically don't have access to theater as well. Shows range from $16 to $20, but some productions are a little less, about $12.

Northwest Children's Theater
1819 NW Everett St.
(503) 222-4480 (tickets), (503) 222-2190 (information)
www.nwcts.org

Northwest Children's Theater is a top-notch production and education group, producing frequent and clever shows that mostly star children. Shows range from interpretations of classic fairy tales such as *Snow White* to adaptations of popular children's books to musicals such as *Annie* to *Hamlet* to original works, all performed with incredible professionalism. Most tickets are in the $15 to $20 range, but there are some great shows for $5. These productions are as entertaining for adults as they are for the children, so don't be a snob.

Oregon Children's Theater
Portland Center for the Performing Arts
(503) 228-9571
www.octc.org

This professional theater company has residence at the Portland Center for the Performing Arts, primarily showing at the Winningstad and Newmark Theatres. They adapt children's classics such as *James and the Giant Peach*, *A Wrinkle in Time*, and *How I Became a Pirate*; they also produce original works. Tickets fall into the not-so-cheap range, but the first time you go to the theater, you can participate in their "First Timer First Saturdays" program, which offers children's tickets for $5, with the purchase of a regular priced adult ticket, on the first Saturday a show is in production. You can also reduce costs by skipping the Ticketmaster fees and buying directly from the box office (you should do this in advance).

Tears of Joy Theater
Portland Center for the Performing Arts
(503) 248-0557, (360) 695-3050
www.tojt.com

Tears of Joy is an amazingly inventive puppet theater performing at the Winningstad Theatre. Their shows are beloved by children but sophisticated enough for adults. You might be surprised at how much pathos *The Ugly Duckling* in puppet-theater has. Tickets are in the $15 to $18 range, but they also host a number of special events that cost less than $10.

THEATER **FESTIVALS**

Fertile Ground
http://fertilegroundpdx.org

Fertile Ground is a fringe festival with a very Portland twist: All the works produced are from local writers, on the theory that this will keep the artistic and financial benefits here in the city. Part of the reason this works is that this festival of new works is put together collaboratively, with just about every theater arts organization participating in the readings, workshops, interviews, and world-premiere full productions. It's held during the last part of January and beginning of February. You can buy a season pass for $50, a "discount" button for $5 (to get reduced prices at some events), or see many events for free, especially readings of new works. Full productions will cost more, of course.

JAW
Portland Center Stage
Gerding Theater
128 NW 11th Ave.
(503) 445-3700
www.pcs.org

Hey Kids! Let's Put on a Show!

I have seen shows in London and New York, but one of the best theater experiences I ever had was seeing a Cleveland High School production of Steven Sondheim's *Into the Woods*. Why? Because the play was about the experience the high school student actors and their parents were actually having—the processes of growing up and letting go. This real-time drama unfolding before us on the stage was powerful indeed, maybe in some ways more so than if the show were put on by Actors Equity professionals. High school productions have a beautiful rawness to them that transcends any imperfections in their productions, and you don't have to be related to the cast members to enjoy these shows. High school productions are also great for introducing children to theater experience and etiquette. High schools with drama departments usually have 3 productions each year, including student-produced one-acts. Ticket prices are usually $10 to $12. The following high schools in Portland and Beaverton have notable drama departments, and this is by no means an exhaustive list.

Portland
Cleveland: www.pps.k12.or.us/schools/cleveland
Grant: www.pps.k12.or.us/schools/grant
Jesuit High School: www.jesuitportland.org
Lincoln: www.pps.k12.or.us/schools/lincoln
Roosevelt: www.pps.k12.or.us/schools/roosevelt
Wilson: www.pps.k12.or.us/schools/wilson

Beaverton
Arts & Communications Magnet Academy: www.beaverton.k12.or.us/acma/deptTheatre.htm
Beaverton High School: www.bhsdrama.org
Southridge: www.beaverton.k12.or.us/home/schools/southridge
Sunset: www.sunsetapollos.org

The Catch: Admission is free, but spaces are limited and fill quickly.

Each July, Portland Center Stage keeps it fresh with a summer playwright festival, JAW (for Just Add Water). This 2-week event has readings of new plays, a theater fair, performances, parties, dance events, and other delights, with free admission to everything. Most events are first come, first served. The festival also includes a unique opportunity to witness and even participate in playwriting, acting, and directing workshops by nationally known artists. These "Community Artists Labs" are also free, but because seating is limited, tickets are assigned by lottery. If you want to see one of these, you'll need to get on the list (available on the website, above) and cross your fingers.

DISCOUNT **TICKETS**

Chinook Book Deals
http://pdx.chinookbook.net

Purchasers of the Chinook Book (Portland's local coupon book; see the Shopping chapter) can get 2 tickets for the price of 1 from a number of production companies, including Portland Center Stage, Portland Playhouse, Lakewood Theatre Company, Third Rail, Artists Rep, and others.

Goldstar.com

The Catch: Note that the tickets, while half-price, will incur a service fee.

Goldstar.com sells half-price tickets to local theater productions (and everything else, for that matter). When an event's organizers realize they need to fill some seats, they will release tickets through Goldstar so they can have a full theater and you can see some great shows at a discount. You do need to become a member, which is free, and tolerate e-mails from them, but this is a small price to pay for the large discounts.

FILM:
CHEAP SHOTS

"Oh, you're a director?
Jimmy, our busboy, is a director!"

—MICHAEL VARHOL, CHRISTOPHER GUEST,
AND MICHAEL MCKEAN, *THE BIG PICTURE*

The film industry likes Portland. While our cinemascape is not as iconic as New York's or as versatile as Toronto's, Portland has been the backdrop for a lot of movies, from Gus Van Sant's *Drugstore Cowboy* to Rob Reiner's *Stand by Me* to the inaugural of the Twilight series. But that's not why the film industry likes us. It's because we have one of the highest rates of per-capita movie-going around, with 66 theaters and 331 screens. For that reason, we have a lot of choices—many independent films, international films, and underground films are shown here, and sometimes made here. Perhaps because of the long, dark winters, Portland has contributed to the phenomenon of re-creating the home-viewing experience at local pubs and restaurants. An entire industry has grown up around making people feel at home while watching movies—at home, but better, because the projection and sound are better and you don't have to wash the dishes. This trend began at local pubs showing second-run movies and serving beer—a cheap bastard's dream come true. Read on to find out more.

INDEPENDENT **THEATERS**

Portland has a robust independent theater scene, including old cinema houses lovingly refurbished and restored as well as vintage theaters serenely basking in their fading, glorious glamour. These theaters—many of them family owned—offer first- and second-run movies at great prices, as well as sponsor festivals and events. They are not always as plush as their corporate chain sisters, but they are great bargains, with large screens and tastier popcorn. Please note that many of these theaters are cash-only.

Academy Theater
7818 SE Stark St.
(503) 252-0500
www.academytheaterpdx.com

The Academy Theater reopened to rave reviews in 2009 after being closed for nearly 40 years. This gorgeous venue has 3 screens, comfortable reclining seats, and excellent sound. You can enjoy your first-run film with delicious pizza from Flying Pie and a beer—or sushi and organic juice if you prefer. They also serve popcorn, ice cream, and organic chocolate, because it is Portland, after all.

Ticket prices typically run $4 for adults, $3 for children 12 and under and for those over 65. They accept credit cards. The Academy has some great specials in addition to their normal low prices. Tuesday you'll find 2-for-the-price-of-1 tickets, but Monday's special is our favorite. You can see 2 consecutive movies for $6 (or $5 if you are a child or a senior)—without the guilt imparted by sneaking into the movies.

Because they serve alcohol, the Academy requires anyone younger than 21 to be accompanied by an adult. But they do have family-friendly, all-ages "after-school specials." They also offer reasonably priced babysitting for movies before 8 p.m. Thurs through Sun. (You'll need to reserve a time and fill out a release form.)

Note: Parking in the Montavilla neighborhood may require patience. Don't park in back of the theater in the Vinje & Sons Heating & Cooling parking lot. You will be towed and it will cost you $250 to get your car back. That is not cheap! You can always take the #15 bus, which lets you off 1 block away. There is also a bike rack.

Cinema 21
616 NW 21st Ave.
(503) 223-4515
www.cinema21.com

Cinema 21 is on the high end of the bargain theaters, with ticket prices at $9 ($7 for matinees), $8 for students, and $6 for children and seniors—and sometimes higher for special events. However, it is one of the few places you can see art films, cult hits from Asia, and sing-along spectacles such as *Grease* or *Mary Poppins*. We love Cinema 21 for its big screen and consumer-tested seating. A special dispensation from the Oregon Liquor Control Commission allows them to serve alcohol but permits all ages at all shows, which is really excellent for the *Grease* sing-along. You can buy tickets online (or at the box office).

Cinemagic
2021 SE Hawthorne Blvd.
(503) 231-7919

Cinemagic—which does not have a website, though they do have a Facebook page—is a friendly neighborhood theater specializing in first-run films at mouthwateringly reasonable prices. They also feature independent and international films. We don't mind the creaky seats at all, and it's close to a number of great bars and cafes. Tickets are $4.50 before 6 p.m. and $6.75 after 6 p.m. Cash and checks only.

Clinton Street Theater
2522 SE Clinton St.
(503) 238-8899
www.clintonsttheater.com

This lively theater is ground zero for the Portland underground film scene—it actually sponsors PUFF, the Portland Underground Film Festival—every spring. But in addition to its cinematic avant-garde, it also shows family favorites such as *Ace Ventura, Pet Detective*. You can just never tell what you'll find. Tickets are $6; $5 for students; $4 for seniors; matinees are $4; and on Tuesday, all shows are $4. If you can find appropriate material, children can see films for $3. *The Rocky Horror Picture Show* still shows every single Saturday night at midnight, since April 1978. All shows after 7 p.m. are for those 21 and over (except *Rocky Horror*). Cash only.

Hollywood Theatre
4122 NE Sandy Blvd.
(503) 281-4215
www.hollywoodtheatre.org

The Catch: $4 tickets can be had only with annual membership in the organization. The lowest price membership is $25 for students and seniors, and $35 and up for everyone else. Membership benefits also give you some discounts to special events.

The Hollywood Theatre is a vibrant cultural center in the heart of the Hollywood neighborhood and a large part of its soul. You can see movies in its beautifully restored glory, but the Hollywood Theater is way more than that: it offers classes, workshops on making movies, training, volunteer opportunities—and, for the right projects, financial support for emerging filmmakers. All this, and Red Vines and M&Ms (and popcorn and beer) too. Ticket prices range from $4 to $7. Monday night shows are $5.

Laurelhurst Theater and Pub
2735 E. Burnside St.
(503) 232-5511
www.laurelhursttheater.com

The Laurelhurst Theater is a beautiful 4-screen establishment that features first- and second-run films, classics, and documentaries at the sweet, sweet price of $3 per show for adults 21 and older. On weekend afternoons, children accompanied by an adult can see the matinee shows; children's tickets are $1. (All shows after 3 p.m. are for ages 21 and older.) They will accept Mastercard and Visa for you frugal people racking up airline miles. And they have a great menu of microbrews, pizza, wraps, salads, and the usual movie accoutrements. In spite of the age and time constraints, the Laurelhurst is very family-friendly, with lots of great all-ages matinees. Taking your kids to see *Harry Potter and the Deathly Hallows* for $1 on the big screen is maybe worth waiting for.

Living Room Theaters
341 SW 10th Ave.
(971) 222-2010
www.livingroomtheaters.com

The Catch: No discounts for 3-D movies, which range from $10 to $12. And the $5 discount price does not apply on public holidays.

The Living Room Theater (the plural above is due to the fact that there is also one in Boca Raton) takes the cinema pub to its logical conclusion. Instead of lounging on vintage couches in an old-fashioned parlor, you curl up in sleek seats in what feels like a private screening room to see the latest in independent films, special broadcasts, and international premieres, as well as the best of the 3-D offerings. Everything is gorgeous and design-y, with an eye toward zero waste and sustainability. Instead of pizza and beer, you'll find grilled ahi and a frosty Caipirinha. This part is not cheap. Ordinary movie ticket prices are also not cheap: $9 for a regular ticket, and $7 for a matinee. Students and educators get in for $6, and seniors for $5. But on Monday and Tuesday, everyone gets in for $5. That's the cheap part.

Moreland Theatre
6712 SE Milwaukie Ave.
(503) 236-5257

When we go to the movies, more often than not we just go see what is playing at the Moreland Theatre—from *The King's Speech* to the latest Harry Potter, whatever they've booked, it's usually good. While it's not the place to see the newest 3-D extravaganza, we love this beautiful old movie palace, run by some nice and very friendly owners, for its first-run movies at beautifully reasonable prices (about $5 per ticket) and yummy cheap popcorn and other concessions. We even like the local advertising they run before the previews. They don't have a website, but you can see what's playing if you Google the name of the theater or if you check www.portland.mrmovietimes .com. Parking can sometimes be challenging—there's a bit of a bottleneck at the intersection of Milwaukie and Bybee—so give yourself an extra few minutes. Bring cash.

Northwest Film Center
1219 SW Park Ave.
(503) 221-1156
www.nwfilm.org

The Northwest Film Center sponsors films throughout the year. This school offers a broad curriculum of filmmaking, screenwriting, and similar classes that can lead to a certificate of film study. The film center also houses a media arts resource center, and happily for the rest of us, it is also a terrific conduit of current and classic art and foreign films. Costs for classes vary depending on length and topic. Call the center for more information on tuition. Every year the center sponsors 3 major festivals: the Portland International Film Festival (see Film Events); the Northwest Film and Video Festival featuring work by regional filmmakers, animators, and cinematographers; and Young People's Film and Video Festival. We really like the Northwest Film Festival because it not only showcases local talent, but it also brings in important independent filmmakers, such as Todd Haynes, Gus Van Sant, and Matt Groening, and it is more low-key than PIFF. The center also sponsors an unusual festival devoted to sound and vision: the Reel Music Festival. Films are usually screened at the museum's Whitsell Auditorium, Southwest Park and Madison. This center represents less frugality than many venues, but it features things that are harder to come by, so the basic laws of capitalism are at work. Tickets are $9, $8 if you're a member of the Portland Art Museum, a senior, or a student; and $6 if you're a member of the Film Center itself. Double features are $3 more.

Portlander Cinema

10350 N. Vancouver Way
(503) 345-0300
http://portlanderinn.com/entertainment/cinema

Many of the independent movie theaters in Portland show experimental cinema in older theaters that while beautiful are, let's face it, showing their age. Then there is the Portlander Cinema, in the Portlander Inn complex at the Jubitz Travel Center (that is, truck stop) on I-5. This is not like that. They show first- and second-run movies for $3, in comfortable, modern seats with surround-sound and climate controls. (There is also a truck museum in the complex, in case you want to visit that too.) Take exit 307; you can't miss it.

Roseway Theater

7229 NW Sandy Blvd.
(503) 282-2898
http://rosewaytheater.com

The handsome Roseway Theater is the only restored movie house in town that offers digital picture and sound—and 3-D. You can buy tickets online and pick them up at the theater. They don't have the usual discounts— ticket prices are $7 all seats, all show times—except for 3-D movies, which are $9. But that's still a lot cheaper than paying for 3-D in the movie theaters at the mall.

Valley Cinema-Pub

9360 SW Beaverton Hillsdale, Beaverton
(503) 296-6843
www.valleycinemapub.com

This family-friendly, locally owned cinema pub offers $4 tickets for all shows. Shows beginning at 5 p.m. and after serve alcohol, so minors need adult accompaniment and aren't allowed in after 7 p.m.—except for Monday, which features "matinees" all day. The space is vintage 1960s, making it the youngest sibling in the old theater family. It tends to be chilly, so bring a sweater. Sometimes they have really incredible specials, like pre-paying for family matinees, so the price works out to be about $1 per show.

McMenamins Theater-Pubs: Beer and a Movie

Mike and Brian McMenamin are two brothers who began as brewers but ended up as real estate developers and community creators. One of their visions was to create neighborhood venues that the whole family could enjoy while mom and dad were having a pint. They were the first in Oregon to pioneer the cinema pub—a place where you could watch a movie and have a beer.

All of their cinema pubs have comfortable seating, good sound, and excellent projection. Some, like the Mission, St. Johns, and the Bagdad, are actual theaters that have been reclaimed. Others were designed for other things and have had theaters installed. A superb example is the Kennedy School—the brothers renovated an abandoned school, reclaiming classrooms and offices to create a comfortable hotel that has become destination for much of Portland. The Kennedy School is very popular for meetings, reunion dinners, parties, and all manner of gatherings—including the movies.

Schedules are updated each Wednesday. Some venues have first-run films; others have second-run films and special events. Movies are $3 per person; minors must be accompanied by adults and are not permitted for the evening shows. For more info, check out their website at http://mcmenamins.com.

Bagdad Theater
3702 SE Hawthorne Blvd.   Movie Line: (503) 249-7474 x1

Edgefield Power Station Theater
2126 SW Halsey St., Troutdale   Movie Line: (503) 249-7474 x2

Kennedy School Theater
5736 NE 33rd Ave.   Movie Line: (503) 249-7474 x4

Mission Theater
1624 NW Glisan St.   Movie Line: (503) 249-7474 x5

St. Johns Theater
8203 N. Ivanhoe St.   Movie Line: (503) 249-7474 x6

ALTERNATIVE **THEATERS**

99W Drive-In Theatre

Hwy. 99W, west of Springbrook Rd., Newberg
(503) 538-2738
www.99w.com

The Catch: This is not a great option if you don't have a lot of toddlers with you—there is a minimum vehicle charge for a single person of $12.

So, driving out to Newberg might not be the most cost-effective way to see a movie, and the prices are on the higher side of the bargain menu, but you can bring your own popcorn, which mitigates the cost a little. And let's face it: Drive-ins are fun. Prices are $8 for adults, $4 for children 6 to 11, $4 for seniors, and zero for anyone 5 and under.

FREE **MOVIES**

Portland has two kinds of free movie nights: indoors and outdoors. From time to time, local cafes, bars, and restaurants will run free movie nights—sometimes according to a theme and sometimes eclectically. These series come and go according to the energy and attention of the proprietors. However, two such series have been reliable over the years, at Pix Patisserie and at Old Town Pizza. And during the summer, when no one can resist staying outdoors as long as possible, there are several varieties of free movie nights.

INDOOR FREE MOVIES

Pix Movie Night

3901 N. Williams Ave.
(503) 282-6539
www.pixpatisserie.com/pages/news-events

The Catch: It is a cafe, so the movie is free, but you should order dessert. If you answer the trivia question correctly, you could win a macaroon, however.

Each Monday night, the delightful Pix Patisserie shows free movies at 8:30 p.m. These range from the comic (*Clueless*) to the sublime (think *Babette's Feast*), from the frightening (*Amityville Horror*) to the classic (*Casablanca*). You just don't know what you will get.

Monday Night Movies
Old Town Pizza
5201 NE Martin Luther King Blvd.

This series runs every Monday night at 8 p.m., with a variety of films for all ages. Sometimes there are extensive series, with many unusual offerings—and a well-known Martin Luther King Jr. Film Festival in January. Get there by taking the #6 or #72 bus (or drive or bike).

OUTDOOR FREE MOVIES

Summer Movies in the Parks
www.portlandonline.com/parks
(Click on the Recreation tab and scroll down to "Summer Free for All.")
Each summer, Portland Parks & Recreation offers 2 series of free movies: Dive-In Movies and Movies in the Park. These are very popular—they combine 3 things Portlanders love: their parks, their summer evenings, and their movies.

Movies in the Park
The Catch: Sometimes it rains. Portland Parks will let you know via Twitter and Facebook by 5 p.m. if they are going to cancel a particular event.

In 2011, Portlanders had 44 opportunities to see a movie under the stars. Movies are shown throughout city parks and public places on different evenings, with a surprising amount of variety. The screens are 268 square feet. The sound system is good. Be sure to bring blankets or lawn chairs and dress warmly—it can get chilly in the evening. The offerings include classics as well as more recent releases, and sometimes you'll find special events such as silent films with live music or sing-alongs. One year, the parks department took advantage of a serendipitous solar eclipse to show *Twilight: New Moon*.

Dive-In Movies

During summer evenings, Portland Parks & Recreation offers outdoor showings of popular movies (often with a watery theme: think *Finding Nemo*). Dive-in Movies are shown at outdoor pools across the city on giant screens, inviting families to float about in the water as they watch favorite flicks. The pool water is heated to extra warm temperatures, which is great because Portland summer evenings can be cool. Usually, the same film plays at different locations during different weeks of the summer. Show time is 8 p.m. You don't have to be in the pool—you can sit on the deck as well. Be sure to keep an eye on the little ones. For a schedule, visit the Portland Parks website at www.portlandparks.org and click on Summer Free For All.

The Catch: You have to pay for the pool admission—adults $5, and youth (3 to 17) $3 (children younger than 3 are free). And . . . you are watching movies in a swimming pool. If you are a true cineaste, this forum will not be for you.

Flicks on the Bricks
Pioneer Courthouse Square

This free Friday-night film series of family-friendly films makes excellent use of "Portland's Living Room," Pioneer Courthouse Square. While there is plenty of seating on the brick benches of the square, you might be more comfortable with a smaller camp chair. Movies begin at dusk, usually starting in July, when the weather is more reliable.

FILM **EVENTS**

Portland International Film Festival

The Catch: PIFF does not have many volunteer opportunities, unlike many similar festivals across the country. You can see movies pretty cheaply if you support the center through memberships, starting at $75. If you lay out $300 for the "Director Level" membership, you can get into all the film festival showings for free. The more you contribute, the more free stuff you get—tickets to non-festival films, invitations to screenings and to hobnob with important filmmakers, etc. Like everywhere else, money buys access here. But if you really like the movies, this could be a good investment.

The Portland International Film Festival (PIFF) brings 3 weeks of movie madness, seeming to grow larger every year. It is by far the biggest film event in Oregon. Expect to see a variety of professional, experimental, traditional, and avant-garde films—as well as lectures, talks, and exhibits. There are fun events complementing the festival, such as filmmaker salons in local bars. The opening and closing nights feature the Portland premieres of new major movies, and if you lay out some dough ($10 to $25, depending on your status), you can be "invited" to the parties that accompany them. Admission fees are $10 per film, unless you are a level-one pass holder ($7), a student or senior ($9), or under 12 ($7).

DANCE:
CHEAP MOVES

"There are shortcuts to happiness,
and dancing is one of them."

—VICKI BAUM

Something about the weather in the Northwest seems to encourage dancing—maybe it's because you can do it inside, out of the rain. In any case, all over the city, people are dancing their hearts out, and you can watch them—or dance yourself—cheaply. You will find all varieties of dance in Portland, both to practice and to watch, and you will especially find innovative choreography. Maybe it's the connection to Burning Man, maybe it's our hipple roots, but there are a number of companies who specialize in trapeze and stilt work as well as plenty of jazz, modern, African, and ballet. We also attract fire dancers, who come here in the off season, where it's nice and damp.

PERFORMANCE

Bodyvox
1201 NW 17th Ave.
(503) 229-0627
http://bodyvox.com

This company has an international reputation for witty, expressive, and joyful choreography, the kind that makes you wish you could start your life over and be a dancer. To see them cheaply is a bit of a feat in itself, however. Your best bet is to watch for their free outreach events, which are advertised on their Facebook page and their website. Bodyvox also has community events such as free ballroom dance instruction on International Dance Day (April 29). They have a robust menu of classes, as well.

Do Jump!
Echo Theater
1515 SE 37th Ave.
(503) 231-1232
www.dojump.org

Do Jump! is noted for its physical theater, distinctive choreography, and—mostly—for its aerial acrobatics. There are few things as thrilling as watching dancers soar out over the audience, believe me. They perform at the Newmark, downtown, but their home is a simple theater just off Hawthorne

Boulevard. Here you can see them cheaply by attending the many student recitals and other workshops that are offered throughout the year, which are $10 and under or even free. You might even sign up for a class yourself.

Jefferson Dancers
www.pps.k12.or.us/schools/jefferson-dancers

The Jefferson Dancers are absolutely the best way to see awe-inspiring talent, sheer physicality, and embodied expressiveness at reasonable prices in Portland, or anywhere. This company is a preprofessional group from North Portland's Jefferson High School; when you watch them soar through the air for 2 hours on end, it's hard to remember that they are high school students. They are not only exceptional in their physical performance, but also in their choreography—these students work with some of the most talented choreographers in the US and beyond. One year they did a dance on skis (it was called "Skia"—seriously, check it out on YouTube). Jefferson Dancers perform regularly. At least once you should try to attend their beautiful recital held every year at the Portland Center for the Performing Arts; tickets for this springtime gala are not terribly expensive, but the online ticketing fees almost double the cost. But these are high-school students, so they also perform recitals in their high school, and for these, the top-priced ticket is $6. Go, now.

Oregon Ballet Theatre
818 SE 6th Ave.
(503) 222-5538
www.obt.org

The Oregon Ballet Theatre, under the direction of renowned artistic director Christopher Stowell, presents classics such as *Petrouchka* and *The Nutcracker*, and they are committed to showcasing new choreography as well. Significantly, most of their performances use live, rather than recorded, music. And they have a highly regarded ballet school. All of this means that tickets are not cheap! Fortunately, they have numerous community events throughout the year at which you can see dancers at work and participate in workshops; many of these events are cheap or free. They include Fertile Ground in January (see the Theater chapter) and Dance Talks, among others. Also of note is that they schedule many *Nutcracker* performances, and it is possible to get discounted tickets to these performances if they don't sell out.

Polaris Contemporary Dance Center

1501 SW Taylor St.
(503) 380-5472
www.polarisdance.org

Polaris is an innovative dance troupe with a beautiful space in Southwest Portland. Seeing them for free or cheap is difficult but it can be done. These community-minded dancers often participate in festivals such as JAW, as well as helping out nonprofits such as Mercy Corps in their fund-raising endeavors. You can find out about these options by following their website. Otherwise, your best bet is Goldstar.

The Portland Ballet

6250 SW Capitol Hwy.
(503) 452-8448
http://theportlandballet.org

We love the Portland Ballet—this excellent ballet school provides some of the best deals for viewing dance and introducing your children to it. They have recitals as well as full-on productions of classics such as *Swan Lake*. (Incidentally, they also have an excellent dance program for male dancers.) Tickets are usually about $10 for adults and $5 for children and students.

White Bird Dance

5620 SW Edgemont Place
(503) 245-1600
www.whitebird.org

This longtime Portland dance ensemble was an early adopter of the avant-garde choreography that put Portland on the map. They host many other companies and collaborate widely. They also create innovative choreography and sponsor education and outreach programs for the Portland Public Schools and other groups. As with most of the other companies in Portland, it is hard to see them cheaply—as with Polaris, your best bet is to see them through their outreach programs.

DANCE **INSTRUCTION**

While the companies listed above offer instruction for jazz, ballet, and other classical forms at various levels, sometimes you just want to get over your nerves so you can practice your *Dancing with the Stars* routine or not embarrass yourself at your wedding. You can get some help cheaply with the companies below.

The Ballroom Dance Company
8900 SW Commercial St., Tigard
(503) 639-4861
http://theballroomdancecompany.com

The Ballroom Dance Company, in Tigard, has cheap dance parties every week; these include at least 30 minutes of instruction and are open to the public. Ballroom, west coast swing, and Latin dance parties are held on Sunday ($5). West coast swing is also offered on the third Friday of the month, with an hour of instruction ($7). On the third Saturday, they have a teens-only dance ($8 for an hour lesson plus snacks).

Portland Dancesport
7981 SE 17th Ave.
(503) 236-8160
www.portlanddancesport.com

The Portland outpost of this international dance-instruction chain offers a multitude of private and group classes in every ballroom dance style—and a reputation for taking the clumsiest of dancers and transforming them into graceful partners in an atmosphere of kindly encouragement. To participate in this goodness cheaply, you can attend drop-in and open classes: Wednesday night salsa practice for $5 (even better, this is free if you take the $12 salsa class before), and Thursday night open ballroom dancing for free! Of course, you'll get hooked and want to take the classes. Nothing is really free, is it? If your kids are interested in ballroom dancing, they can attend age-appropriate drop-in classes for $8 per session as well.

Viscount Dance Studios

724 E. Burnside Ave.
(503) 226-3262
www.viscountstudios.com

Viscount Dance Studios is a great dance-instruction studio that offers classes in African and other interesting forms, as well as traditional ballroom-style dancing. On weekends, they have fantastic dance socials for cheap. Students and the public can get a little dance instruction and then practice, practice, practice in a safe environment, all for the grand sum of $5. They even provide snacks. Classes rotate from salsa to swing to Bollywood to tango and are suitable for all ages.

MUSIC:
OF THEE I SING

"If it sounds good, it is good."

—DUKE ELLINGTON

Music is one of the art forms that Portland does well—there are low entry barriers (you don't need a whole theater, just a corner at the farmers' market) and it is rewarded at every level by a DIY ethos. Portland has become home to many indie-band musicians escaping Los Angeles or Seattle, so evidently I am not the only person who thinks this. For that reason, the music life in Portland is incredibly rich, and that means it might be free to you, since there is so much of it.

KEEPING **UP:** LOCAL **MUSIC** NEWS

We have a number of fantastic and easy ways to know what is going on in the Portland music universe at any given moment. My very favorite is **Portland Concert Co-op** (http://portland.concertcoop.com). This online calendar is incredibly useful—it allows you to do filtered searches of local music events, so you can peruse all the free or $5 shows on any given day. You can further filter by all-ages, genre, area of town, and so on. It is a very well-designed tool.

The traditional sources of information (i.e., print) are also great, in part because Portland Concert Co-op doesn't have every venue in it (although it has many, many of them). You can read the dead tree or online versions of the *Oregonian* (www.oregonlive.com) or *Portland Monthly* (www.portland monthlymag.com), both of which have excellent coverage of the cultural scene. For music other than classical, probably your best bets are print or online versions of either the *Portland Mercury* (www.portlandmercury.com) or *Willamette Week* (www.wweek.com/Portland), which are passionate about covering the local music scene. Passionate. *Willamette Week* is so passionate they created a whole festival, just so they could write about more things (see Musicfest Northwest, below). I would also like to point out that the *Mercury* and *Willamette Week*, which are both alternative weeklies—rival weeklies, at that, making things fun for readers—are both free.

FAVORITE **VENUES**

Aladdin Theater
3017 SE Milwaukie Ave.
(503) 234-9694
www.aladdin-theater.com

The Catch: Ticket fees apply *($2 for plastic, $1 for cash or check) even when you buy directly from the box office.*

The Aladdin Theater is an old-fashioned venue seating about 600 that feels something like a high-school auditorium—and I mean that in the best possible way. It's intimate enough to allow a great connection between the audience and the performer, which really heightens the experience for both. Both the great and the obscure play here. Tickets tend to cost less here than at many other venues in town; many shows are in the $12 to $15 range. You can buy from the box office directly, which is the best way to avoid the Ticketmaster fees. They'll still charge fees, but far fewer of them.

Artichoke Music
3130 SE Hawthorne Blvd.
(503) 232-8845
www.artichokemusic.com

Artichoke Music is a music store that also provides a fantastic venue for performing and listening to the best in folk music. They have a stage with frequent performers, which may or may not cost, but they also have fun ways to hear music for free. On Thursday, they host the "Songwriters Roundup," where you can test out your newly written music on someone else; Friday night they hold a coffee house; and Saturday holds a jam session.

Biddy McGraw's Irish Pub
6000 NE Glisan St.
(503) 233-1178
www.biddymcgraws.com

Biddy McGraw's is a nice Irish bar that has an outstanding and frequent lineup of great music—not just Irish, but also bluegrass, rock, folk, gypsy blues, singer-songwriter, and the gamut. They also have many all-ages shows. Usually, there's no cover, or not much of one, although this depends on the performer.

Blue Monk
3341 SE Belmont St.
(503) 595-0575
www.thebluemonk.com

The Blue Monk is a jazz-plus venue with a variety of music events that are often, though not always, free. Sunday night they have an excellent jazz series featuring local, regional, and sometimes national acts; the cover for this series starts at $3. I've never seen anything higher than $7, and sometimes the cover is on a sliding scale.

Crystal Ballroom
1332 W. Burnside St.
(503) 225-0047
www.danceonair.com

The Crystal Ballroom is a huge venue, now with a related hotel across the street, that has several bars and stages. The main feature is the ballroom itself, outfitted with gizmos under the dance floor that make the floor roll and shake a little, so that you feel that you are either dancing on air or in an earthquake, depending on how many beers you have had. The sheer variety of shows here makes it valuable to keep an eye on—anything from a $5 cover to see 5 local bands to $30 to see Iron & Wine.

The Doug Fir Lounge
830 E. Burnside St.
(503) 231-9663
www.dougfirlounge.com

The Catch: All shows are for those who are 21 and older.

The Doug Fir is one of the best places to see live music in Portland. Not only is it good-looking, but it was also created especially to showcase live music: The stage and the sound system are both top-tier. Shows here range from the famous to the obscure and are priced accordingly—that is, you can see 3 sick new bands for $5, though you might pay $15 to see Menomena. Buying in advance is usually cheaper, unless it's for the $5 shows.

Holocene
1001 SE Morrison St.
(503) 239-7639
www.holocene.org

With 2 stages, Holocene is a great venue for live music (and DJ'd dancing too)—it has a cool modern bar and plenty of room to dance. The drinks are generous. The live-music cover is priced right. I once saw a secret show by M. Ward here for $5 with my friends Cara and Houston, delighting our cheap little hearts as well as our ears.

Jackpot Records
209 SW 9th Ave.
(503) 222-0990
www.jackpotrecords.com

Fabulous Jackpot Records keeps going strong, even in the age of the download—now they not only sell records, but they have become a record label themselves. But the reason you are reading this book is to find out what they can do for you, cheaply. And here is the answer: they hold in-store events with bands such as the Decemberists and Franz Ferdinand, as well as newly emerging talent, that you can go see, for free. A second location is at 3574 SE Hawthorne Blvd. (503-239-7561).

Laurelthirst Public House
2958 NE Glisan St.
(503) 232-1504
http://mysite.ncnetwork.net/res8u18i/laurelthirstpublichouse

Laurelthirst features lots of local bands playing folk, roots, bluegrass, jazz, and other genres, but besides the fine music, the teeny stage makes the music experience chummy. Covers are cheap, and the beer, wine, and cocktails are thirst-quenching.

Mississippi Studios
3939 N. Mississippi Ave.
(503) 753-4473
www.mississippistudios.com

Mississippi Studios is a recording venue that also acts as a very intimate performance space and for that reason is a really fun place to see a show, since you are practically sitting in the band's lap (or vice versa). You might be surprised at the quality of artist who performs and records here—besides talented indie bands from Portland, you might see Rickie Lee Jones or Freedy Johnston. It's also attached to a lovely bar, Mississippi Station. Ticket prices vary—and they do have $5 and free shows.

Music Millennium
3158 E. Burnside St.
(503) 231-8926
www.musicmillennium.com

Music Millennium is a fabulous and large record store that carries every genre—including possibly the best classical CD collection in the west—and is staffed by friendly and knowledgeable people. In addition to all of this competence, they sell concert tickets and have their own in-store events. Sometimes these events cost money, but other times they are free.

Press Club
2621 SE Clinton St.
(503) 233-5656
www.myspace.com/thepressclub

The Press Club is a French-style cafe specializing in crepes and amazing sandwiches, as well as wine, coffee, and cocktails. They are known for their impressive wall of periodicals. By day, people sip coffee and read *Interview* or the *New York Review of Books*. But at night it's a different story. The Press Club hosts many live music and other events in its intimate space, most of which don't even have a cover charge. A crowd favorite is Swing Papillon, which plays beautiful gypsy jazz on Wednesday night for free.

CLASSICALLY **CHEAP**

Classical music is not always cheap, but there are some surprising bargains to be found. One critical resource is Portland's excellent classical music radio station, **All Classical FM** (www.allclassical.org), KQAC. This commercial-free station, which has an international following, is the best resource for classical music events in the area. They have free ticket giveaways, as well as up-to-date information.

Metropolitan Youth Symphony
(503) 239-4566
www.playmys.org

The Metropolitan Youth Symphony has a full symphonic orchestra as well as numerous ensembles, all staffed by student musicians, from middle grades to young adults. That does not diminish their quality, however—they have a full repertoire of exciting pieces. A regular concert venue for them is the Arlene Schnitzer Concert Hall; here tickets can be fairly cheap depending on the seats, but the fees are hefty. But they also play elsewhere in the community, and tickets can be as low as $5 to these other events. Check their website for updated events.

Oregon Repertory Singers
909 SW Washington St.
(503) 230-0652
www.orsingers.org

The Oregon Repertory Singers, who also have a robust youth choir program, focus on a wide range of classical and contemporary works, including ones that sometimes fly under the radar. They will often work with groups such as the Portland Baroque Orchestra, presenting fresh interpretations of familiar favorites by Bach, Handel, Mozart, and company. Cheap tickets (about $10) are available if you are okay with back-of-the-house seats.

Oregon Symphony
923 SW Washington St.
(503) 228-1353
www.oregonsymphony.org

The Oregon Symphony, the oldest west of the Mississippi, has an incredibly loyal following, in part because of its excellence and in part because of the charisma of its leaders. The principal conductor is the European-trained and Uruguayan-born Carlos Kalmar—he also heads the Grant Park Music Festival in Chicago. In 2011, he brought the symphony to Carnegie Hall for the first time ever. You can see this popular conductor and his exciting orchestra for free in early September each year, when they perform their annual outdoor concert at Tom McCall Waterfront Park. The program varies, but it always ends with Tchaikovsky's *1812 Overture*, complete with fireworks.

Portland Chamber Orchestra
(503) 771-3250
www.portlandchamberorchestra.org

The Portland Chamber Orchestra is a nimble 35-piece orchestra that is noted for its beautiful interpretations of favorites such as Handel's *Messiah* and their work with soloists, such as Lindsay Deutsch, as well as local talents. Normally, season tickets to concert series are not such a deal, but these are almost too good to be true. Regular season tickets are $65; for seniors, $55; students, $45; and children, $15.

Portland Youth Philharmonic
421 SW Hall St.
(503) 223-5939
www.portlandyouthphil.org

One of the best ways to hear live classical music cheaply is to look to its youngest practitioners. Portland Youth Philharmonic was established as the first youth orchestra in the US, tracing its origins to the Sagebrush Symphony, which was founded in 1912. This amazing organization has 2 full symphony orchestras and a third orchestra for younger students. You can hear them at the Arlene Schnitzer Concert Hall—not all the tickets are cheap, but some of them are as low as $10 for adults, depending on the show. They also precede the Oregon Symphony at their annual free concert (see the entry above on the Oregon Symphony).

Sherman Clay Pianos
131 NW 13th Ave.
(503) 775-2480
www.shermanclay-portland.com/piano-concert-events

Sherman Clay Pianos presents monthly piano concerts—their showroom doubles as a performance space—and similar events that are usually free. Some of these include student recitals and recitals from local luminaries, while others feature nationally and internationally known pianists. They have an e-mail newsletter that will keep you apprised of such events. This is a fine venue for piano music, especially when it's free.

COMMUNITY **MUSIC**

Community Music Center
3350 SE Francis St.
(503) 823-3177
www.communitymusiccenter.org

Run by the Portland Parks office, the Community Music Center is a hub of preprofessional and amateur musical activity of all varieties. The center is housed in a beautifully restored 1912 fire station, but you would never know the building's original purpose if you were sitting in the acoustically excellent concert hall. Community Music Center events are mostly free, and there are many of them—many recitals, for one thing, but also free concerts such as the Family Fridays series, which brings in professional musicians. The recitals vary in their level of quality—sometimes it's beginning violinists. But sometimes it's a talented pianist practicing for a Van Cliburn competition. That's one heck of a free show.

Blending Community & Music

One of the best ways to see local bands is at two popular markets: the Portland Farmers' Market and Saturday Market. At the Farmers' Market, you will find a couple of stages with local performers—most of the offerings are bluegrass, folk, and indie-root music, in keeping with the spirit of the market. You will also find kids busking in every acoustic genre you can think of, and some of this music is incredibly good. **The Farmers' Market** (www.portlandfarmersmarket.org) takes place at Portland State University from Mar through Dec, Sat 8 a.m. to 2 p.m. **The Portland Saturday Market** (it also runs on Sun; www .portlandsaturdaymarket.com) sells tie-dyed T-shirts and sand-cast candles, but it also features many performers, many of them musical, and many of them for children. They blend in seamlessly with the organized chaos of the market. Saturday Market is open from the first weekend in March to Christmas Eve. On Sat the market begins at 10 a.m. and closes at 5 p.m.; Sun hours are 11 a.m. to 4:30 p.m.

Vespers at Trinity Cathedral

Trinity Episcopal Cathedral
147 NW 19th Ave.
(503) 222-9811
www.trinity-episcopal.org

From October through May, on the first Sunday of every month at 5 p.m., the exceptional chamber choir of Trinity Cathedral offers a vespers service and organ recital featuring a guest organist on their gorgeous Rosales mechanical-action organ. This evening prayer service is surprisingly popular in unchurched Portland. Trinity's choir is well known for its gorgeous interpretations of classical and contemporary choral music and is now led by renowned director Michael Kleinschmidt. They also sponsor many other music events and concerts throughout the year, many of which are also free.

FESTIVALS & **CONCERT** SERIES

FREE

Summer at the Square
www.pioneercourthousesquare.org

Portland's Pioneer Courthouse Square has free concerts at noon on Tues and Thurs in July and Aug. These concerts feature an eclectic range of music— jazz, folk, rock, folk rock, you get the idea—from talented Northwest artists. What could be better than eating your bento in pretty Pioneer Courthouse Square on a gorgeous July day listening to a cool singer songwriter? How about doing that for free?

Summer Free for All
Citywide, various locations
(503) 823-PLAY
www.portlandparks.org

There are few better ways to watch a long summer evening come to a close than to sit in a lovely park watching the light soften and listening to some great music. Portland's Parks & Recreation office sponsors free concerts during July and August throughout a number of the city's many parks. You can find a concert somewhere nearby almost every weeknight. Check the website for times, bands, and locations.

CHEAP

Chamber Music Northwest
Various locations
(503) 223-3202, (503) 294-6400 (tickets)
www.cmnw.org

Chamber Music Northwest is one of the nation's premier chamber music festivals. Artist-director David Shifrin gathers together renowned soloists and ensembles for an inspired summer series (there are also events throughout the year). Guest artists have included such stars as Bill T. Jones, the Orion Quartet, and Anne-Marie McDermott, among many others, and the festival also includes numerous lectures and outreach events. One of these is the Protégé series, which features young, up-and-coming artists in performance, held in casual spaces such as coffeehouses—and these events are free. This is a fantastic way to get the family behind the idea of chamber music. In addition, some discounts are available for the regular concert series: Senior rush tickets can be purchased for $20 when available (30 minutes prior to the show); students 7 and older pay $15 per ticket; and if you are a PSU student, faculty, or staff member, you can attend any event at Lincoln Hall for free, provided you arrange it in advance.

Musicfest Northwest (MFNW)
http://musicfestnw.com

A number of years ago, local alternative weekly *Willamette Week* got tired of just writing about things and decided to put on a show. The result is MFNW, which features 250 bands and takes over 20 stages around town for 3 fantastic days of musical multitude. The main stage events happen at Levi's Pioneer Stage at Pioneer Courthouse Square. That's where bands like the Decemberists, Wiz Khalifa, and the Smashing Pumpkins play to dancing crowds. But the festival unfolds all over the city. You can buy a wristband and see everything (not cheap!); you can also purchase tickets at the door of the various venues, and these vary in price—anywhere from $5 to $20-plus. The main stage tickets at Pioneer Square cost more than $30—but it is an outdoor show in the middle of a city. Just saying.

Portland Jazz Festival
Various locations
(503) 228-5299
http://pdxjazz.com

The Portland Jazz Festival is held in February to coincide with Black History Month. This thematically organized festival invites some of the best jazz musicians in the country, as well as featuring local stars. Sometimes in a happy coincidence, these are one and the same—for example, Dave Frishberg and Esperanza Spalding. This festival lasts a week, and while some of the tickets are uncheap, there are numerous free events throughout. Some of these are education forums and lectures, but you will find many fabulous free performances as part of the festival.

Waterfront Blues Festival

Tom McCall Waterfront Park
(503) 282-0555
www.waterfrontbluesfest.com

Fourth of July weekend marks the first weekend of summer for Portlanders—it seems to stop raining for the year on July 5—and the Waterfront Blues Festival provides the soundtrack. This festival hosts some of the best jazz and blues artists in the region and in the nation, with several stages and 4 days' and nights' worth of music. It's very popular, to the point that people anchor their boats off the seawall to enjoy the festival with more privacy (and, I suppose, no admission fees). Admission is cheap—$10 plus 2 cans of food for the Oregon Food Bank. The festival does a good job of closing off most of the waterfront such that you practically must enter the festival. But you can still find spots outside the gates but close enough to the stage that you can hear, if you are desperate. One bonus: On the Fourth of July, the festival includes fireworks as well.

READINGS & OPEN MICS:
FREE EXPRESSION

"Reading is a discount ticket to everywhere."

—MARY SCHMICH

Portland is a readerly town, which is entirely unsurprising when you consider the weather. The evidence is everywhere: Powell's City of Books, which is the largest independent bookstore in the country, as well as a number of other fantastic independent bookstores; Portland Arts & Lectures, in which people pay a premium to hear writers lecture at them, for fun; Wordstock, a fabulous literary festival very much in the Portland spirit; two well-respected literary magazines; a store devoted to 'zines. All of this activity means one thing for you: somewhere in the city, there is an entertaining literary reading for you, one that is really cheap or altogether free. Many of these events are held at our excellent independent bookstores, which you should frequent and buy books from if you want to keep going to free readings.

REGULAR **EVENTS**

With so many open mics, readings, and other literary events happening in Portland, it's good to have a guide to the ones you can count on.

"Comma"
Broadway Books
1714 NE Broadway
(503) 284-1726
www.broadwaybooks.net

Broadway Books, a lively and far-sighted independent bookstore in Northeast Portland, hosts a monthly reading series on the third Thursday from 7 to 9 p.m. This series, called "Comma," is organized by local polymath Kirsten Rian—she's a fine artist, writer, photographer, teacher, and rock and roller—and showcases 2 regional authors each month. This event is followed by an open mic, if you want to be a regional writer too.

First Wednesdays
Blackbird Wine—Atomic Cheese
4323 NE Fremont St.
(503) 282-1887
http://blackbirdwine.com

One of our stellar literary magazines, the *Oregon Literary Review*, hosts readings and other performances from area writers, musicians, and storytellers. Many of these are renowned Oregon artists, while others are new voices. Wine tasting is also available, making the event that much more entertaining. First Wednesdays take place, naturally, on the first Wednesday of each month, from 7 to 9 p.m.

Mountain Writers

The Press Club
2621 SE Clinton St.
(503) 233-5656
www.myspace.com/thepressclub
www.mountainwriters.org

Mountain Writers is a longstanding writers' community that offers incredible workshops, retreats, and access to some of the most important writers in the US. Their faculty and guest speakers include important writers such as Sharon Olds, Dorianne Laux, Carl Adamshick, and Judith Barrington. The workshops and special events are not so cheap, but every third Wednesday, the writers in residence and other community members host readings at the wonderful Press Club. Readings are free, and the beer, wine, and coffee are not expensive unless you want them to be. Events begin at 7:30 or 8 p.m. (check the website). This series is excellent, and the Press Club is an intimate setting for it.

Multnomah County Library

Various locations (see Appendix C)
www.multcolib.org

The Multnomah County Library makes the hearts of all cheap literary types beat just a little faster—not only can we check out books, DVDs, and CDs, and even download music for free, but we can also go to all kinds of readings and book-related events, all across the city. Most of these events are free. They have great book discussions and reading groups as well—for example, Books to Action, a reading group dedicated to transforming the community by combining the reading group experience with targeted volunteer projects. Another event is Verse in Person, held at the NW Thurman branch on the fourth Wednesday of the month at 7 p.m. Oregon poets read and discuss their work.

Star E Rose

2403 NE Alberta St.
(503) 249-8128

The Star E Rose is a bustling cafe on NE Alberta, and they love to put readings, storytellers, and poets on their busy events calendar. The best way to find out about these stellar events is to check their Facebook page (Star E Rose Cafe). Events are free or cheap; plus, there's good coffee and pie. They have open mic events as well.

3 Friends Mondays: Caffeinated Art

Three Friends Coffee House
201 SE 12th Ave.
(503) 236-6411
http://showandtellgallery.org

Every Monday evening, two or three artists show up at the Three Friends Coffee House and make beautiful music, poetry, comedy, theater, or some other form of performance art together. You just never know what will happen at this fun reading. Show and Tell Gallery hosts this collaborative event every Mon, from 7 to 8 p.m. It's followed by an open mic.

Keeping up with
Literary Events—Reading Local: Portland

With so much going on in the Portland literary universe, it's challenging to keep up. That's where **Reading Local: Portland** is of infinite value. This newsy blog is full of interviews, publishing updates, and events related to books and reading in Portland. The blog fills a critical gap as newspapers and other local media shift their attention and resources. This blog provides a simple way for authors and publishers to promote author events, but even better, it serves as a targeted encyclopedia of bookstores, readings, local literary entities, and resources for writers, readers, and publishers alike. Reading Local has been successful enough in Portland that it is busy launching a network of similar websites across the US, allowing us to think globally while reading locally. You can find and subscribe to Reading Local: Portland at portland.readinglocal.com.

READINGS **AT** BOOKSTORES

One of the ways that bookstores are remaining viable is by hosting literary and other events to remind you that even in the age of e-books—which you can buy in bookstores—we all need a little human interaction. And what could be more human than discussing books with the writers who wrote them? The bookstores below have readings, book groups, and other events, so that every day and evening in Portland, you will find some free literature-related event. Look at their websites or read Reading Local to see what's up.

Annie Bloom's Books
7834 SW Capitol Hwy.
(503) 246-0053
www.annieblooms.com

This longtime Portland favorite has a great online store, a chatty newsletter, and some terrific free writer events. Their calendar is easy to use, and it's right on the front page.

Barnes & Noble
Lloyd Center
1317 Lloyd Ave.
(503) 249-0800
www.barnesandnoble.com

Area Barnes & Noble bookstores have many events for all ages, including story times for children and reading groups for adults. There are actually 6 stores in the area, though the Lloyd Center location is the most central in Portland proper. To see events here or anywhere in the area, click on the store locator tab on the website listed above. This Lloyd Center shop also features a Starbucks and free Wi-Fi.

Broadway Books
1714 NE Broadway
(503) 284-1726
www.broadwaybooks.net

In addition to their "Comma" series, noted above, Broadway Books has many other events, signings, groups, and other forms of literary entertainment.

The staff of this shop has a good ear for events, as well as being incredibly well informed and articulate.

Cosmic Monkey Comics
5335 NE Sandy Blvd.
(503) 517-9050
www.cosmicmonkeycomics.com

Why should serious literature have all the fun events? Cosmic Monkey also has popular author signings, and while you won't be sitting still for a couple of hours listening to someone read, isn't that kind of the point? Check their website for the calendar. Free comics are available the first Saturday of May, which is National Free Comic Book Day.

Excalibur Comics
2444 SE Hawthorne Blvd.
(503) 231-7351
www.excaliburcomics.net

This large comics outlet on Hawthorne—they have millions of comic books, manga, graphic novels, DVDs, and other paraphernalia—also sponsors events. They hold fund-raisers, participate in the annual tradition of Free Comic Book Day, and have author events and book signings. These are almost all free.

In Other Words
8 NE Killingsworth St.
(503) 232-6003
www.inotherwords.org

Portland's proudly feminist and alternative bookstore has been featured in several memorable episodes of *Portlandia*. Do not fear: The staff will help you find the books you want. In Other Words has many readings, classes, and other free or low-cost events (and for viewers of *Portlandia*, no, they won't make you pay to use the bathroom either).

Murder by the Book
3210 SE Hawthorne Blvd.
(503) 232-9995
www.mbtb.com

This fun bookstore is devoted to mysteries of all kinds—they specialize in series and are diligent in keeping them intact. They regularly invite authors to talk, sign books, and read from their latest. Their website has a good calendar.

Powell's Books
Flagship store: Powell's City of Books
1005 W. Burnside St.
(503) 228-4651
www.powells.com

What can we say about Powell's and its place in the hearts of cheap Portlanders? It's the largest bookstore in the country that is in a physical place, and it has a growing online presence. Powell's is well known for its impressive collection, its knowledgeable and friendly staff, and its genuine "third place" sense, which has developed organically and did not need to be manufactured. This giant bookstore in a reading city is a magnet for writers, of course, and every day and night you can find events on the Powell's calendar—at the main store on Burnside but at all the other stores as well. The great majority of these events are free. Readings and signings are targeted to all ages, and the store is open every day of the year. Their online calendar is user-friendly and informative, and if you look at the events section, you'll see a page for Portland-specific information that nicely pulls together things that you would need if you lived here (e.g., how to sell your books at the store, as well as the latest events). The branches of Powell's on Hawthorne (Powell's Books on Hawthorne, 3723 SE Hawthorne Blvd., and Powell's Books for Home and Garden, 3747 SE Hawthorne Blvd.) and in Beaverton (Powell's Books at Cedar Hill Crossing, 3415 SW Cedar Hills Blvd., Beaverton) are worth visiting for author events: They are smaller stores, giving you a more informal experience, all for free. A fifth location is at 40 NW 10th Ave.

Reading Frenzy
921 SW Oak St.
(503) 274-1449
www.readingfrenzy.com

Reading Frenzy is kind of the antithesis to Powell's—small and focused rather than large and sprawling. It features an amazing collection of 'zines, DIY publications, alternative literary quarterlies, and other literary ephemera, and you can consign your vintage 1990s collection of *Temp Slave* or other materials. In addition to all of these nice things, you can also attend their events for free.

CHEAP **READINGS**

Loggernaut
Ristretto Roasters
3808 N. Williams Ave.
www.loggernaut.org/readings

This series, like several others, invites writers to share the stage with one another, which makes for some magical chemistry. Readings are cheap, $2 per person; recently they have been held at the delightful Ristretto Roasters, but check the website. Dates and times vary.

Portland Arts & Lectures
Arlene Schnitzer Concert Hall
1037 SW Broadway
(503) 248-4335
www.literary-arts.org

The Portland Arts & Lectures series, sponsored by Literary Arts, is a tony event that hosts the most influential writers and thinkers in the US and beyond. Those who appear have usually won Macarthur Fellowships, the National Book Award, Pulitzers, and other important awards and prizes. And there is nothing cheap about these tickets, which sell for nearly $300 for the series. Even individual tickets are expensive, about $50. Volunteer opportunities are sporadic. You can, however, see some of these lectures for half price using Goldstar.com. You'll need to keep an eye out, since some events will sell out (and hence there's no need for the Goldstar system).

Tin House Writers Workshop
Reed College
3203 SE Woodstock Blvd.
www.tinhouse.com/writers-workshop

Tin House is a beautiful literary magazine and press that may be better known outside of Portland than in town—their other office is in Brooklyn—and features the writing of major talent such as Mike Sacks, Mary Otis, and Dolly Freed, to mention just a few. Each summer, they hold a distinguished writing workshop with important and successful writers, a workshop that includes evening readings and hobnobbing, a workshop that is anything but cheap. But you can participate in some of it: You can audit portions of the workshop. Individual seminar tickets are $15, and individual readings are $5, or $20 for the whole evening series. Readings and workshops are held on the Reed College campus.

Wordstock: A Book and Literary Festival
Various locations and the Oregon Convention Center
(503) 549-7887
www.wordstockfestival.com

Wordstock is Portland's major literary festival. This fantastic happening includes readings, lectures, teachers' workshops, workshops for kids, music, films, discussions, play readings, dances, interviews, demonstrations, and anything else that is remotely literary. More than 200 writers, over 100 exhibitors, and thousands of attendees converge upon the Oregon Convention Center and other venues throughout the city—coffee shops, grocery stores, the library—to participate. Headline events are not cheap (though they aren't horribly expensive either, about $25) but there are many, many free events as part of this festival. You can join the mailing list to get e-mail updates or peruse the website for the daily offerings; they also produce a printed catalog. Wordstock takes place in the beginning of October, as the bite of fall grows a little sharper, reminding us that the long gloom ahead will be much lighter if we fortify ourselves here and come away with a list of things to read.

GRAB **THE** MIC

If you ever get tired of just reading about things, you might try writing about them instead. And when you do, on any given night, you can share what you've written with someone other than your dog or your children.

Portland Poetry Slam
Backspace Cafe
115 NW 5th Ave.
(503) 248-2900
www.backspace.bz

Portland was an early adopter of the Poetry Slam, and this event has had different incarnations over the years. Recently, it has been held every Sunday at an all-ages cafe, the Backspace. Sign-ups start at 7:30, and the slam is for a $50 prize and the chance to compete nationally. Details can be found on the Portland Poetry Slam Facebook page or at the website above. A $5 donation is suggested.

Open Mics Around Town
Besides keeping up with Reading Local, check out the really useful open mic calendar at http://poetry.openmikes.org/calendar/or. This is a good resource because cafe owners don't always get around to updating their listings when their plans change, and this calendar points out when information has not been updated in awhile. Another resource is Portland Poets Exchange, a Facebook page that maintains a comprehensive list of open mics. Both of these resources are good, but do be sure to check the website, MySpace, or Facebook page of anything you read about (or call them) because the open mic landscape is an especially unstable one. Finally, check out two of the best open mics mentioned above: Three Friends Coffee House, 201 Southeast 12th Avenue, after 3 Friends Caffeinated Mondays; and Star E Rose, 2403 NE Alberta St., which has a long list of events in any given week, a number of which are open invitation.

SECTION 2:

Living in Portland

FOOD:
CHEAP EATS

*"Food is our common ground,
a universal experience."*

—JAMES BEARD

Portland has a growing reputation as a gastronomic destination. It is ideally situated at the north end of the fertile Willamette Valley and the west end of the Columbia River, close to some of the best vineyards in the US, to fresh seafood, and to lush seasonal crops. This regional bounty has drawn some of the nation's most talented chefs here. In the past decade, these chefs and their dining public have fallen in love with each other. The level of excellence in ordinary restaurants is world class; in turn, the ordinary diner has an ever-increasingly sophisticated and adventuresome palate.

Portland is pretty much all about the food these days. The level of activity around and attention to food is remarkable. It's a large-scale experiment in making daily life better using food, wine, and other ingredients from surrounding regions, and the result is that the standards for what you find in an average cafe are much higher than anywhere I have seen in the US. The *New York Times* calls it a "golden age of dining" in the city, and even in this economy, visitors from all over the world flock here to sample the bounty from the Willamette Valley, which is being brought to the table in ever more inventive and succulent ways. And the best part is that it is still possible to eat well very cheaply. Did I say possible? I meant easy.

The idea here is to save money while sampling some of the finest cuisine in the US, although we have included plenty of less exalted fare for the times when you want to be low key. The meals and snacks below range in price from free to about $10. (Also see Downtown Cheap Eats & Drinks map on p. x.)

HAPPY **HOURS**

There are many outstanding food-focused happy hours in Portland—in fact, it's one of the best ways to experiment with restaurants and get a feeling for where you might like to spend more money. Or not. It's up to you. Here are some of our favorites—though this is by no means an exhaustive list. There are many, many places to find happy-hour chicken strips and jojos, but the listings below take it up a notch. Why settle for anything less?

Bar Avignon

2138 SE Division St.
(503) 517-0808
http://baravignon.com

Bar Avignon is a chic and spare spot known for its thoughtful wine list and excellent small plates of things like tangy local cheeses served with honey or succulent fresh oysters with champagne mignonette—as well as fried chicken. Happy hour is 4 to 6 p.m. Mon through Fri, with both drink specials and food specials in the $3 to $6 range.

Biwa

215 SE 9th Ave.
(503) 239-8830
http://biwarestaurant.com

Biwa is an izakaya-style Japanese restaurant: Rather than sushi, the focus is on small plates and noodle dishes. Small plates are always good for those dining on a budget, and the ones at Biwa are especially savory and delicious. Popular dishes include octopus salad, pork belly skewers, gyoza, and hanger steak. Also delicious is a salad made of cabbage rolls, carrots, and daikon radish in a tahini-based dressing, as well as onigiri, which are small sandwiches stuffed with rice and nori. But Biwa is really known for its noodle dishes, especially the pork ramen. Happy hour prices are outstanding: onigiri for $1, hanger steak and pork belly skewers for $2. Late-night happy hours include ramen for $5, with savory add-ons such as pork for a couple of dollars more. Early happy hours are 5 to 6:30 p.m. and late-night hours are 9 to 10 p.m., and until 11 p.m. on Fri and Sat.

Ciao Vito

2293 NE Alberta St.
(503) 282-5522
www.ciaovito.net

Ciao Vito serves attentively prepared traditional Italian fare using Northwest ingredients, and it is one of our favorites. Chef Vito de Lullo has an outstanding happy hour menu that not only includes cheap house wine, beer, and cocktails but also superb, mouthwatering dishes such as pork sugo and fried meatballs for $5 or $6. Even the spaghetti aglio e olio is infused with the perfect amount of spiciness from the peppers and crunch from the bread crumbs—for about $4. And you can enjoy these things for amazing happy hour prices every single day—4 to 8 p.m. on weekdays, 4 to 6 p.m. on Fri and Sat, and on Sun all day. Yes, that is right: all day.

Clyde Common
1014 SW Stark St.
(503) 228-3333
www.clydecommon.com

Clyde Common, in the Ace Hotel, is an ideal spot for an after-work happy hour—it's convivial without being overwhelming and the food is some of Portland's best. Both their traditional fare such as radishes with butter and salt and their more adventuresome offerings like french fries served with harissa, which are making my mouth water just writing about them, receive rave reviews that are well deserved. Their scotch and bourbon list and house cocktails are also outstanding. They have double-shift happy hours, the first being Mon through Fri from 3 to 6 p.m. and then again from 11 p.m. until closing. Happy hour menu items are culled from the overall menu or are made specially, but prices level off after $6. Happy hour cocktails and featured wines are $5; beer specials are $3.50. On Sun, bottles of sparkling wine are half off, all day.

Huber's
411 SW 3rd Ave.
(503) 228-5686
http://hubers.com

The Catch: There's a $3 drink minimum per person.

True confession: Back when the kids were little, money was tight, and we were bored by the endless days, we would sometimes take them to happy hour at Portland's oldest restaurant, Huber's. This was fun because they served miniature hamburgers for $2, which the kids thought were fantastic. We went right at the beginning of happy hour, when it wasn't crowded; we would sip Spanish coffee, and they would have an early dinner and be trained in how to eat in restaurants. The appetizer prices still start at about $2; there are also drink specials. Happy hour runs from 4 to 6:30 p.m. and from 9:30 p.m. until closing. Prices are not applicable for takeout, so if you thought you could leave the kids in the car and just grab the $2 burgers to go, you can't.

Lincoln

3808 N. Williams Ave.
(503) 288-6200
www.lincolnpdx.com

Lincoln can be uncheap if you are eating a proper dinner there, but luckily, they host a weeknight happy hour so you can go more often. Happy hour is held Tues through Fri from 5:30 to 7 p.m., and they serve delightfully salty fried treats: fritters, fries, onion rings, and popcorn, along with cocktail specials for $5 or $6, and wine and beer specials. There's a rotating menu of other items, such as patty melts or poutine. Happy hour food will set you back anywhere from $1 to $6 per item.

McCormick & Schmick's Seafood Restaurant

www.mccormickandschmicks.com

The Catch: One-drink minimum required ($3.50). Also, no takeout (as if!).

McCormick & Schmick's, which also owns **Jake's Famous Crawfish** (401 SW 12th Ave., 503-226-1419) and **Jake's Grill** (611 SW 10th Ave., 503-220-1850)—and the restaurant at the Heathman Hotel, but who is counting? is now a large national chain. But it started right here in Portland, Oregon. It has a popular happy hour menu from 3 to 6 p.m. and from 10 p.m. to close, with delicious fried things that cost about $2 and many drink specials. Each location features different items—for example, the Harborside (0309 SW Montgomery, 503-220-1865), my favorite because it has the best view, has tacos for $1 every Tuesday and the famous half-pound cheeseburger with fries for $3. Your mileage may vary. Check their website for other area locations.

Portland City Grill

111 SW 5th Ave., 30th floor
(503) 450-0030
www.portlandcitygrill.com

The Catch: Food is deeply discounted, but drinks are not.

The main reason to go to Portland City Grill is for the fantastic view of our beautiful region from the 30th floor of the U.S. Bank Tower. And the best time to do it is during happy hour, when prices are much, much cheaper. The menu runs from $2 to $5 per item. The view is free. On Sun, happy hour starts at 4 p.m. and goes until the place closes; the rest of the week it's 4 p.m. to 6 p.m., and then from 10 p.m. until closing.

Spints Alehouse
401 NE 28th Ave.
(503) 847-2534
http://spintspdx.com

For happy hour, this German-inspired, vibrantly noisy neighborhood pub features different "dirty pretzels"—soft pretzels accompanied by delicious things such as braised pork or served tuna melt style—and house-made sausages for $3 off the regular low price. (Other dishes are also available.) Happy hour is Tues through Sun 4 to 6 p.m. and 10 p.m. until midnight. By the way, while it's called an alehouse, don't overlook the yummy cocktails.

Tanuki
413 NW 21st Ave.
(503) 241-7667
www.tanukipdx.com

The Catch: *This Korean/Japanese restaurant has a lot of rules: no splitting checks; everyone has to buy at least 1 drink; you must understand you are in a noisy bar; children are not allowed; just because something is spicy doesn't mean you can send it back. . . . That said, it's totally worth it.*

For true gourmands, this is one of the best happy hours in Portland. High-end sakes and beers for great happy-hour prices. Little delicious plates of spicy, salty, savory food run anywhere from $2 to $9, depending on the complexity (most are less than $5). Happy hour is every day from 4 to 6 p.m.

Tasty N Sons
3808 N. Williams Ave.
(503) 621-1400
http://tastynsons.com

Tasty N Sons is one of the most beloved restaurants in Portland. It's especially beloved for brunch on the weekends, when waits are long, but it also has a delicious $5 happy hour from 2:30 to 5:30 p.m. One of their happy hour dishes is a bacon cheeseburger for $5 that has been known to entice vegetarians to eat meat again. Happy hour food specials are $3 to $6. It is very popular, but if you manage your expectations regarding wait times, you will be rewarded with some of the best food in Portland.

Trebol
4835 N. Albina Ave.
(503) 517-9347
www.trebolpdx.com

Trebol serves delicious Tex-Mex at its fabulous happy hour, which takes place daily from 5 to 6:30 p.m. and then again from 9 p.m. until closing. Drink specials include margaritas or wine for $5, sangria or mimosas for $4, and food specials that start at $4. The enchiladas are our favorite in Portland, but there are excellent pork sandwiches, quesadillas, flautas, and other good things as well. They also have Taco Tuesday, wherein you can get two tacos, a shot of tequila, and a beer chaser for $10.

Urban Farmer
525 SW Morrison St.
(503) 222-4900
http://urbanfarmerrestaurant.com

The Urban Farmer is one of the restaurants within The Nines hotel, and it is very beautiful and modern and expensive. But the happy hour prices, which are from 3 to 6 p.m. daily and 10 p.m. to closing, are not. Small plates of delightful things like sliders are $4 to $5, oysters are $2, crab dip and cheese puffs, $6. Happy hour might actually be the best way to enjoy this restaurant in terms of value.

Victory Bar
3652 SE Division St.
(503) 236-8755
www.thevictorybar.com

I like to say that Victory is the ideal Portland neighborhood restaurant, because it demonstrates the level of quality that is considered normal for a simple neighborhood bar. It is dark and handsome, and it serves really delicious small plates with a surprising amount of house-made ingredients— they smoke their own trout, make their own bitters, cure their own meat, make their own sausage, and fashion their own super-yummy spaetzle that they sell for about $5 during happy hour. They also have excellent cocktails. Try the Bourbon Ginger. Happy hour is daily from 5 to 7 p.m., with food specials at $3 to $5.

FOOD **CARTS**

The talent for great cooking in Portland has spilled out of local culinary schools such as Oregon Culinary Institute and out of the working kitchens of the city's

pod. But we don't listen to them, because we like that there is enclosed heated seating, a dedicated parking lot, and port-a-potties with hot water—and, of course, excellent and very diverse cheap food. You'll find outstanding coffee and smoothies, lemon pie, cheese steaks, escargot, Korean food, an unbelievable Italian spot (Lardo) with a porchetta sandwich that will haunt you, and, well, you get the picture.

Mississippi Marketplace: N. Mississippi Avenue, just south of Skidmore

This pod was one of the first to evolve out of planning rather than a spontaneous outpouring of culinary entrepreneurialism. It therefore has more seating, silverware, etc. It is very busy on sunny afternoons, with people lined up at fantastic carts such as Garden State, which sells east-coast-style sandwiches and other Jersalicious treats.

Portland State University: SW 4th Avenue and SW Hall

Students, and sometimes professors, really need cheap food. Luckily Portland State has one of the best pods just off campus. Many meat-focused carts are here, like ones devoted to meatball sandwiches or house-cured pastrami.

restaurants, and it cannot be contained. It has to express itself somewhere. Hence, it expresses itself as the best street food in the US. This is because of the food carts, mobile restaurants that serve amazing food outdoors. They are the cheapest way to eat well in Portland. If Portland is a laboratory for inventive food practices, food carts are where the benchwork happens. The quality of the food from these entrepreneurial ventures is generally outstanding, especially when you consider the price. Most items you get at the carts cost less than $10, and often they are less than half that. It's not exactly fast food—sometimes, it's not fast at all—but it is always delicious and cheap.

Carts are usually organized into what we call "pods," which are private lots with clusters of carts. Pods often include big picnic tables under tents, sometimes with heaters, so people can sit down and feast in comfort. As outlined below, the pods have a variety of different food carts, so there will be something to please everyone's palate. Think of it as a DIY food court. Carts also appear in little corners of unused land, at festivals or other regular events such as farmers' markets, and anywhere you can tuck them. Some are truly mobile and use Facebook and Twitter to alert patrons as to their whereabouts. Some have gone on to open brick-and-mortar places as well (it's common for food-related businesses in Portland to begin as a booth in the farmers' market or as a cart in a pod). There are now more than 600 carts in the city, with no signs of growth slowing any time soon. One hears some griping about how the carts are getting fancy and how $7 for a burrito from KOi Fusion is expensive and how back in the old days before they got all legit, carts were way better. But fortunately there are still lots of $4 burritos and $3 banh mi sandwiches and $5 barbecue to choose from. I expect we are in a food cart bubble, but I will happily remain in that bubble until it pops.

The online guide **Food Carts Portland** (www.foodcartsportland.com) is essential reading for the food-cart obsessed. They do a heroic job of keeping up with individual carts, pods, cart-related laws and regulations, businesses, etc. They have a useful map function that identifies pods and individual carts. This is a great service, because as you might imagine, there is some volatility in the food cart world. Listed below are a few of the major pods, but more are being created every week so keep your eyes peeled. There's probably one opening up across the street from you any second now.

As noted above, there are more than 600 carts in Portland as of this writing. Many, many of these are excellent. Below are a very few of our favorites, ones that provide the best value—that means both yummy and cheap.

KOi Fusion
827 SW 2nd Ave.
(503) 789-0848
http://koifusionpdx.com

KOi Fusion began as a mobile cart serving amazing Korean-Mexican barbecue. The burritos are incredible, and the tacos are addicting. We would find out where chef Bo Kwon was going to pull up by following him on Twitter. KOi Fusion has evolved to having several trucks and two semi-permanent residences (SE Division and SE 32nd and downtown at the address noted above), as well as a handy online calendar and a website that's legit. You can still follow him on Twitter, however. Slightly more expensive than other street food, but still way less than $10.

La Jarochita
Taco trucks provide some of the best cheap street food ever, and La Jarochita is one of the best taco trucks in Portland. They make excellent tamales, huraches, tortas, and enchiladas. Almost everything is $5 or less. You'll find them at the original pod, SW Fifth Avenue at Stark.

Nong's Khao Man Gai
With 600 food carts, it's hard enough to choose where to eat, let alone what to eat. This cart makes that choice for you by serving only delicious Thai chicken and rice, served in a sauce made with soy, ginger, and garlic for $6. They are downtown at SW Alder and SW 10th.

Nourishment
We look forward to Saturday, when we can go to the Hollywood farmers' market and get some strong Ristretto Roasters coffee and one of Ramona White's fantastic breakfast burritos for really cheap. Nourishment is open on Sat from 8 a.m. to 1 p.m. The market is on NE Hancock Street between 44th and 45th Avenues.

Off the Griddle
4926 SE Division St.
(503) 989-3908
www.facebook.com/offthegriddle

This is the cart that makes my vegan friends weep with joy—its specialty is vegan and vegetarian burgers (and gluten free where possible) that are prepared with great inventiveness and attention. A vegan "cheese" "burger" with "bacon" will cost you $7.50. Yukon gold fries on the side cost extra— but they are worth it.

PBJ's Grilled
919 NW 23rd Ave.
www.pbjsgrilled.com

Grilled peanut butter sandwiches are some kind of genius, especially when they include bacon or banana or both. The most expensive thing on the menu is a peanut butter sandwich on grilled challah French toast, with bacon, maple syrup, and blueberry jam . . . for $6.

Potato Champion

Our family is addicted to the Belgian-style fries served here—particularly the peanut butter and jelly fries (that is, with peanut satay and raspberry chipotle sauce). Also popular is the Portland version of poutine, the Quebecois dish that combines fries with cheese curds and gravy. The kids queue up for it at 2:30 a.m. when the bars close, paying for it with their last few dollar bills. At Cartopia, Southeast 12th Avenue and Hawthorne.

FREE SAMPLES

If you are reading this book, you probably already know that you can gorge yourself silly at Costco by sampling all the foods they put out there for you to try. In Portland, however, you can also do this at the area's grocery stores and farmers' markets. Bon appétit!

New Seasons Market
Multiple locations
www.newseasonsmarket.com

New Seasons is really quite a cultural force in Portland, transforming the landscape for grocery shopping. New Seasons is our local riposte to Whole Foods—a grocery store that offers local, organic, sustainable foods and other products, but also carries Diet Coke and outstanding takeout. It can be more expensive than discount stores, but it's surprisingly competitive. They have superb customer service, and as part of that, they offer amazing samples and demonstration products. Every weekend, from 11 a.m. to 5 p.m., they feature some delicious food that you can try for free, and these samples are generous, especially when they are featuring local produce, such as their berry festival, which is usually held in late June. They also regularly offer fruit, bread, and other sundry items, as well as wine and beer tastings most afternoons. Check out their website to get information on all area locations.

Trader Joe's

2122 NW Glisan St.
(971) 544-0788
www.traderjoes.com

Trader Joe's is known for its focused, excellent product list—as well as its free samples and demonstrations. They usually concentrate on 2 products in combination, and we usually miss the point of the free samples by buying whatever they are demonstrating (or I guess we take the point, depending on how you look at it). They also have free coffee. Additional Portland locations include 4715 SE Cesar E. Chavez Blvd. (503-777-1601), 4121 NE Halsey St. (503-284-1694), and in Happy Valley at 9351 Southeast 82nd Ave. (503-771-6300).

Portland Farmers' Market

Portland is passionate about its central farmers' market, held Mar through Dec, Sat, 8 a.m. to 2 p.m. at Portland State University (www .portlandfarmersmarket.org). Every Saturday, crowds flock to the market to buy produce, cheese, meats, flowers, and everything else that is grown in the region. They also eat breakfast or lunch, listen to music, socialize with all the friends they run into, take their kids to the balloon man, and generally celebrate the local bounty—including the free samples. Farmers and purveyors from all over the region set up shop, and you can wander from booth to booth nibbling on little bits of cheese or hazelnuts or fresh fruit or lamb sausage or whatever else they are offering. You can also brave the crowds and get the tasty samples from whatever visiting chef is demonstrating chef skills that weekend. Seasonal events also mean lots of free samples—tomatoes, berries, bread, cheese, pumpkins—at least once a month, there's some kind of festival, and that means a snack for you.

But wait! There's more! The Portland Farmers' Market provides just one opportunity to sample regional goodness. From May through Oct, there's a market somewhere in the Metro area pretty much every day. For a complete directory of all farmers' markets in Oregon, go to the **Oregon Farmers' Market Association** website at http://oregon farmersmarkets.org.

Whole Foods
Multiple locations
http://wholefoodsmarket.com/content/portland

It is not nicknamed "Whole Paycheck" for nothing. But Whole Foods does have some great deals. They have generous samples of wine, cheese, pastries, and fruit. And in addition to these delicious samples, Whole Foods has good prepared food that you can take home or eat on site. They have "family meals" that include roast chicken and vegetables, baked ziti, or some other main dish serving four, plus a large salad—all for less than $20. And they have happy hours with seasonal foods and wine. A recent favorite included oysters in mignonette for $1 apiece, plus a glass of excellent Spanish wine for $3. Check out their website for information on all Portland area locations.

CHEAP **FOOD**

Besides free samples and happy hours, Portland has an abundance of really good restaurants that are not expensive. The following are our favorite places to get excellent, excellent food for really cheap! By that, we mean $10 or less for an entrée. You will find a lot of breakfast and lunch places, perhaps not surprisingly, but a good variety of international cuisines as well.

An Xuyen Bakery
5345 SE Foster Rd.
(503) 788-0866
www.anxuyenbakery.com

Banh mi, which are Vietnamese sandwiches on French baguettes, are one of the best ways to eat cheaply in Portland and beyond, and An Xuyen is one of the best banh mi shops in Portland. Banh mi usually includes pickled carrots, daikon radish, and cucumbers, all very thinly sliced, as well as cilantro, mayonnaise, chili peppers, and the primary filling—barbecued pork, sausages, ham, beef, or even tofu, all served on a fresh baguette. Family-run An Xuyen is notable because they supply the baguettes for many of the other banh mi shops around town. A delicious sandwich plus coffee is less than $4, and they also have great steamed buns and other tasty things. Dinner here will be early: They are open only until 6 p.m. except on Sun, when closing time is 3 p.m. But you could get your sandwiches to go.

Best Baguette
3635 SW Hall Blvd.
(503) 626-2288
www.bestbaguettesandwiches.com

Best Baguette serves savory banh mi and sweet bubble tea to west-siders. They are known for their excellent variety—sandwiches are about $3.25, and there are more than 30 to choose from. Try the Saigon bacon with avocado.

Bunk Sandwiches
621 SE Morrison
(503) 477-9515
www.bunksandwiches.com

Every day at lunch, Bunk Sandwiches offers eight beautiful sandwiches— they are not always the same, but they will usually include sausage, pork belly Cubanos, meatball sandwiches, tuna melts, vegan options, and more. This list does not do them justice, however. They have a well-deserved cult following for serving outstanding dishes, and you won't pay more than $10 for the whole meal.

Burgerville
Convention Center
1135 NE Martin Luther King Jr. Blvd.
(503) 235-6858
www.burgerville.com

There are 39 Burgerville drive-ins in Washington and Oregon (the original store is across the river in Vancouver, WA) and this flagship restaurant adjacent to the Convention Center is right in central Portland. In some respects Burgerville is not cheap—a drive-through dinner for four will cost $20, which seems like a lot for fast food. But this local burger joint is still a great value—and its commitment to using local and seasonal ingredients, right down to the Oregon Country Beef and the fresh strawberries for the milkshakes in summer, means that you can feel better about indulging in a bacon cheeseburger. Another plus is that you can get kids' meals with sliced apples instead of french fries. Of course, none of this would matter if

Burgerville's food wasn't also delicious. You can drive through or eat in from 6:30 a.m. to 11 p.m. 7 days a week. This location has free Wi-Fi. Check the website above to find a Burgerville near you.

Country Cat
7937 SE Stark St.
(503) 408-1414
www.thecountrycat.net

The Country Cat is a favorite of Portland gastronomes, but you can enjoy this charming Montavilla restaurant even if you are on a budget. On Monday night, they serve their delicious house burger with a pint of beer for a grand total of $12. On Tuesday, they serve a fantastic pork sandwich with baked beans, and they throw in a couple of shots of Jack Daniels, for $10. Wednesday and Thursday, it's 10 wings plus a beer and fish and chips plus a beer, respectively. And if you are in the industry—and by that I mean the restaurant business—you can get half off your second entrée if you are buying two of them.

Detour Cafe
3035 SE Division St.
(503) 234-7499
http://detourcafe.com

The Detour Cafe serves delicious breakfasts and lunches that are very cheap, and I mean that in a good way. Their sandwiches are superb, especially the succulent Cubano and the mouthwatering BLAT (bacon, lettuce, avocado, tomato) served on house-made focaccia. Your only challenge will be getting a seat. Be patient.

Eugenio's
3584 SE Division St.
(503) 233-3656
www.eugenios.net

This micro-deli serves great espresso and pizza but the real draw is the sandwiches. They use Draper Valley chicken, as well as sausages from local maestro Fred Carlo, who makes the best Italian sausage known to mankind. You'll also find pizza, soups, and salads. Nothing on the menu is more than $10, however.

Fuller's Restaurant
136 NW 9th Ave.
(503) 222-5608

A Portland stalwart, Fuller's serves a mighty breakfast all day until 5 p.m. on weekdays, 2 p.m. on Sat. We love their egg sandwiches, which are cheap. They take cash only—that's how you know how cheap they really are. Closed Sun.

Ha VL
Wing Ming Market Center
2738 SE 82nd Ave.
(503) 772-0103

The Catch: For the best pho in the west, you'll need to have it for breakfast: They close at 4 p.m. and run out of soup long before.

Ha VL has some of the most amazing banh mi sandwiches and Vietnamese soups on the west coast. Soups change every day (no soup on Tues) but they tend to run out before lunch. Favorite soups include spicy pork, curried chicken, and beef pho; you will also find—and should try—traditional tripe, fish (e.g., dried shrimp or crab), and other soups. They feature 2 soups per day.

J & M Cafe
537 SE Ash St.
(503) 230-0463

We love the J & M for many reasons, one of which is the J & M plate, which is like eggs Benedict but better because it is made with thick bacon and uses cheese instead of hollandaise; another of which is the excellent waffle; and another of which is the self-serve coffee. But really, any dish here, from the delicious baked treats to the simple eggs and bacon, will be worth it.

Justa Pasta
1336 NW 19th Ave.
(503) 243-2249
www.justapasta.com

Justa Pasta makes the pasta for many of Portland's finest restaurants, but if you want to skip the linen tablecloths and accompanying prices, you can go directly to the source. They have a small, casual restaurant where they serve lunch and dinner, featuring daily specials comprising several pastas and

The Best Fancy Dinner for Cheap

The best path to fine dining for cheap in Portland is via the **Oregon Culinary Institute,** 1701 SW Jefferson St. This professional cooking school is the only one in town that has a reliable and consistent restaurant where they actually train cooks and front-of-the-house staff. You can go either for the 3-course prix fixe lunch for $9 (seating at noon) or the 4-course prix fixe dinner for $18 (seating at 7 p.m.). The food is generally excellent: It is prepared under the watchful eyes of very experienced chefs. Because it is Portland, students are trained in the culinary ways of the seasonal and local, so the menu is ever changing. For dinner, you will get a starter, a salad, an entrée, and dessert. Wine, beer, and soda are extra, but cheap—about $4 for a glass of very decent red, for example. To make things even better, the Chinook Book has a coupon for Oregon Culinary Institute—buy 1 dinner or lunch, get another free (1 coupon per table, though). Tips go to support their scholarship fund. You do need to make reservations, since there may be times when the school is not in session. To make a reservation, call (503) 961-6200 from 9 a.m. to 6 p.m., Mon through Fri (office hours).

sauces along with bread from the Pearl Bakery and well-flavored salads. We especially love it when they serve butternut squash–hazelnut ravioli, which has a delightful combination of silky and crunchy textures. The raviolis and lasagnas are all delicious, as are the simple noodle dishes such as bucatini in Bolognese sauce.

Nicholas

3223 NE Broadway
(503) 445-4700
http://nicholasrestaurant.com

Nicholas serves delicious and very cheap Lebanese and Middle Eastern food—hummus, falafel, dolmas, gyros, kebabs, shawarma, the freshest possible pita, lentil soup, and so on. Their mezze platters can be ordered to serve up to 4 people (for about $35), but frankly, the 1-person mezza for $9 can be split by 2 people and you will still be perfectly satisfied. In fact, you would still have room for the baklava and fragrant cardamom-spiced Turkish coffee. Two additional locations are at 318 SE Grand Ave. (503-235-5123), and 323 N. Main Ave., Gresham (503-666-3333).

Pho Nguyen
4795 SW 77th Ave.
(503) 297-3389

Pho—Vietnamese noodle soup—is one of the most divine ways to eat cheaply, and Pho Nguyen is one of the most divine pho shops around. This west-side favorite, a hidden gem in a strip mall, serves a mouthwatering chicken pho (*pho ga*), as well as refreshing salad rolls and grilled pork, all with generous portions and friendly service.

Pho Van
1919 SE 82nd Ave.
(503) 788-5244
www.phovanrestaurant.com

Pho Van began as a noodle shop serving the Southeast Asian community in east Portland, but soon the reputation of their beautifully balanced pho broth, salad and hand rolls, curries, and savory grilled meats drew diners from all over the city, and they had to expand. The 3 shops have slightly different menus and emphases, but in all of them, you can get amazing, fragrant beef and chicken pho, as well as other noodle soups such as braised duck with shiitake mushrooms and bok choy. The pho easily feeds 2 people. Rarely are any items on these menus more than $10. Two additional locations are at 3404 SE Hawthorne Blvd. (503-230-1474), and 11651 SW Beaverton-Hillsdale Hwy., Beaverton (503-627-0822).

Pok Pok and Whiskey Soda Lounge
3226 SE Division St.
(503) 232-1387
www.pokpokpdx.com

James Beard Award–winning chef Andy Ricker began Pok Pok as a take-out shack serving northern Thai street food; it now occupies several buildings (and Ricker has gone on to open other restaurants), and even so, there are lines out the door. It is not quite as cheap as in the old take-out days, but you can still order half a perfectly rotisseried guinea hen and sticky rice for $9 and think you have gone to food heaven. The signature dish, these juicy birds are flavored with lemongrass and garlic, covered by a golden, crispy skin. Across the street and down half a block is the Whiskey Soda Lounge (it used to be in the basement of Pok Pok); you can get a pre-dinner cocktail and some shrimp chips there and then head back over to Pok Pok. Or you can just stay at Whiskey Soda Lounge and split an order of Ike's Vietnamese Fish Sauce Wings for $12 and the best Thai noodles you've ever eaten for $8, and call it good. (The noodles at Whiskey Soda Lounge are only available on their late-night menu, from 10 p.m. to close, but the wings are always available.)

Por Que No
3524 N. Mississippi St.
4635 SE Hawthorne Blvd.
(503) 467-4149

Por Que No is very, very, very popular because it is very, very, very good—and cheap. Tacos are probably the best deal—succulent and delicious carne asada, tangy fish, handmade tortillas, fresh guacamole, and salsa. You could spend more money, but why? Be prepared to wait in line, however.

Sapphire Hotel
5008 SE Hawthorne Blvd.
(503) 232-6333
www.thesapphirehotel.com

The Sapphire Hotel offers great value. This pretty bar and restaurant has many different specials and appetizers. We love their antipasti plate, and they also have an excellent weekend brunch with yummy things like Meyer lemon crepes. They also have a taxi fund, which could come in handy on Sunday when they offer bottomless mimosas for $10.

Slappy Cakes
4246 SE Belmont St.
(503) 477-4805
http://slappycakes.com

This bright and bustling diner keeps prices low by having you make your own pancakes right at the table. You order batter by the pint, and then you can order add-ins on top of that—blueberries or dried cherries, for example, or bacon. This has been a very popular gimmick, especially with families—although you will find a diverse crowd, since evidently everyone likes to make pancakes and have someone else clean up. You can also order other food that you don't cook yourself, but it's neither as fun nor as cheap, although it's still pretty good.

Sushi Ichiban
24 NW Broadway
(503) 224-3417

Sushi is something that seems like it should be inexpensive, since each little dish is by itself not so much money. Yet anyone who regularly eats sushi knows that it is an expensive indulgence, since it is hard to eat just one or two little dishes. And the idea of cheap sushi can give you pause, considering how the cheapness might have been achieved. That's where Sushi Ichiban comes in. This downtown sushi-conveyor-belt spot has many fans due to its combination of quality and cheapness. It's not Sasabune, but it is cheap. Plus, the conveyor belt is actually a small train. How cute is that?

Toro Bravo
120 NE Russell St.
(503) 281-4464
www.torobravopdx.com

Toro Bravo is a tapas-style restaurant with a reputation for excellence. To eat there economically—which is a little bit challenging because everything is so yummy—it is necessary to order a round of delicious things such as dates wrapped in bacon, kebabs, and paella, and then hang onto the menu to order more if you are still hungry. Toro Bravo is a very Portland restaurant in that the cuisine and techniques of the Iberian peninsula are interpreted through the lens of the Pacific Northwest and its wonderfully fresh ingredients. So the bacon-wrapped date might also be stuffed with locally sourced foie gras and seasoned with fleur de sel.

Zell's
1300 SE Morrison St.
(503) 239-0196

People go to Zell's for the German apple pancakes, but they stay for everything else—the eggs Benedict, the scones, the corned beef hash. Plus breakfast is served all day until closing at 2 p.m., something of a rarity in Portland. You can eat like a king for less than $10.

DRINKS:
CHEAP BUZZ

*"My only regret in life is that
I did not drink more champagne."*

—JOHN MAYNARD KEYNES

Drinking is fun, but it can be an expensive habit, even if you take it up as a hobby and brew your own. Actually, this approach is almost a guarantee that you will spend thousands more annually than if you just happily drink someone else's stuff. Hence, this chapter is intended to reduce the cost of drinking. It covers wine tasting, beer tasting, and sampling Portland's distilleries. But you should go into this cheap drinking adventure armed with some knowledge. These purveyors are offering free and cheap tastings because they are hoping you will buy some of their products. And you should think about that, because otherwise they can't keep giving you free booze. It's good karma, for example, to be open to purchasing wine at a wine tasting, especially because you are establishing a relationship with the vendors, and maybe even the winemakers. And reciprocity is important for any healthy relationship, even if you are cheap.

Portland has a culture devoted to the handmade, the local, and the unique, and this culture extends from the vineyards to the breweries to the local bars that sell cocktails with locally made rum and homemade bitters. With such abundance, it's easy to find cheap drinks of every variety (check out the "It's Five O'Clock Somewhere" sidebar, on p. 87). The listings here focus on added value, whether that's becoming more educated, having access to more variety, or offering something unusual. (Also see Downtown Cheap Eats & Drinks map on p. x.)

WINE **TASTINGS**

Cork • A Bottle Shop
2901 NE Alberta St.
(503) 281-2675
http://corkwineshop.com

This shop has many events, from classes to traditional tastings. Many of these events are gloriously free, and they happen at different days throughout the week, rather than the typical Fri or Sat. They also happen to have well-priced wines for $20 and under.

E & R Wine Shop
6141 SW Macadam Ave. # 104
(503) 246-6101

E & R specializes in European wines, especially Italian wines. (Once I ran into one of the owners at a wine festival in the hill town of San Gimignano in Tuscany, so I know they do their research.) The owners are low-key in person, but they have a funny newsletter that is a pleasure to read, and that's where they will tell you about their great wine-tasting events.

Every Day Wine
1520 NE Alberta St.
(503) 331-7119
www.everydaywine.com

This friendly wine bar in Northeast Portland wants to demystify the wine-drinking process, so they offer informative tastings in the $10 to $15 range. They also have good values for you to take home. Notably, they don't have a predefined wine list, so if you drop by for a glass of wine, you can try almost anything (for a price, of course).

Foster and Dobbs
2518 15th Ave. NE
(503) 284-1157
http://fosteranddobbs.com

Foster and Dobbs is a shop featuring artisanal cheese and other small-batch food, but they also have an excellent wine and beer collection, and they have free tastings on Friday afternoons. It's one of the few places in town you can sample gourmet pickles with high-end vermouth. Most of the tastings focus on wine, but they do have beer sometimes too.

Great Wine Buys
1515 NE Broadway St.
(503) 287-2897
greatwinebuys.com

This shop has attentive service along with their wonderful selection of Northwest, California, and European wines and wine accessories. Friday night tastings are more upscale and require a larger cash outlay and sometimes reservations and prepayment; Saturday tastings are casual and free.

Korkage Wine Shop
6351 SW Capitol Hwy.
(503) 293-3146
http://korkagewineshop.com

Korkage has a regular $10 Thursday evening tasting that goes from 6 to 9 p.m.—several hours later than most of the wine shop tastings. They also have happy hour from 4 to 6 p.m., Wed through Fri, and live music on Fri. And they offer small plates of food, which will make your visit less cheap, but perhaps more convenient.

Liner & Elsen Wine Merchants
2222 NW Quimby St.
(503) 241-9463
http://linerandelsen.com

Liner & Elsen is routinely voted as one of the top wine shops in a city of excellent wine shops. They have special events that usually carry a $10 glass fee. They have fee-based tastings on the first and third Friday of each month, at which they pour a 5-wine flight. (For more cash, you can get a "super-pour."). These tastings are not super-cheap, running from $10 to $15. But on Saturday, the tastings are free, starting at noon and continuing until they run out or to 5 p.m., whichever comes first. Saturday tastings tend to feature international wines, which is good in a city that can be self-absorbed.

Mt. Tabor Fine Wines
4316 SE Hawthorne Blvd.
(503) 235-4444
http://mttaborfinewines.com

At $15 for their 5-flight tastings, Mt. Tabor is not the cheapest place for sipping wine, but they do have some amazing deals—although you could always buy the wine without tasting. They are specialists in the Oregon pinot noirs (as well as in Burgundies for the Francophiles out there) for which the Willamette Valley is so justly renowned.

Portland Wine Merchants
1430 SE 35th Ave.
(503) 234-4399
www.portlandwinemerchants.com

We love this shop—it fits in with the DIY ethos of Hawthorne, offering excellent prices on closeouts and odd bottles as well as a well-edited wine collection from all over. You can visit them for their $15 Friday night tastings, or you could visit on Saturday and Sunday and see what they are pouring, for free.

Storyteller Wine
5511 SW Hood Ave.
(503) 206-7029
www.storytellerwine.com

This wine shop has many interesting events, and among them are free tastings on Friday. (Sometimes there are tasting fees, so do check the website first). They sell most of their wines online, so these events are extra fun, maybe because sitting in front of a computer all day makes you long for company. They invite local and distant winemakers to hobnob with their devoted followers.

Thirst Wine Bar & Bistro
0315 SW Montgomery St. #340
(503) 295-2747
www.thirstwinebar.com

This charming spot along the Willamette has an excellent view of the river—and free wine tastings on Thursday from 5 to 8 p.m. A heavenly thing to do on a summer evening.

Vino
137 SE 28th Ave.
(503) 235-8545
http://vinobuys.com

The people who run Vino could not be nicer or have yummier wine. Plus they want to share it with you—on Friday night, they have wonderful $10 tastings of well-curated wine collections. On Saturday and Sunday, they like to share inexpensive wines for free, to keep you coming back for more. Another excellent feature is that Vino is across from the outstanding Ken's Artisan Pizza, which you should try. It is not cheap, but if you've been sipping delicious free wine, you might not really care.

Vinopolis
1025 SW Washington St.
(503) 223-6002
www.vinopoliswineshop.com

This is the largest wine shop in Portland—which means good deals for you, if you can bring yourself to buy something nicer than Two-Buck Chuck. (They have online specials too.) Vinopolis has tastings and special events— the cheaper ones tend to start at about 3 p.m., with 4-flight pours for $5. They have also been known to open bottles for random tastings, so you could stand around looking hopeful.

BEER **TASTINGS**

Oregon is home to 87 breweries and counting, and Portland claims to have more microbreweries per capita than anywhere else in the country—in other words, it's Beervana around here. This means that on any given weekend, there will be a festival, tasting, or other beer-related event, and some of these will be free or very cheap. One good source for tasting events is the calendar maintained by the **Oregon Brewers Association:** http://oregon beer.org/category/beer-tasting. You should also note that July is Oregon Beer Month—there are several different festivals organized at this time, as noted below—so watch for even more specials.

Bailey's Taproom
213 SW Broadway
(503) 295-1004
baileystaproom.com

Bailey's Taproom is one of the best places to sample beer in Portland—they have 20 taps that rotate frequently, as well as an impressive bottle list. Plus, they are very friendly and love to talk about beer. Their samplers are a great value—$7.50 for five 5-ounce pours. You can also get a 10-ounce pour for $2.50. Bailey's is in a handsome open space with an industrial-chic feel, and they have a lot of board games, so it is fun for a cheap and interesting date.

Belmont Station

4500 SE Stark St.
(503) 232-8538
http://belmont-station.com

This bright and bustling Southeast institution not only sells you beer, but it also wants to educate you. Thus, they have well-organized and numerous events throughout the year where you can meet brewers from the area and beyond, learn about different regional styles, and sample beers for free. Check out their events page—there is something new all the time.

Cascade Brewing Barrel House

939 SE Belmont St.
(503) 265-8603
www.cascadebrewingbarrelhouse.com

The focus here is on Belgian-style sour beers, many of which have fruit as an essential component even though they are not at all sweet. I guess we have reached a point in Portland beer culture where you can be this specialized, and that is telling us something. In any case, this handsome little pub on Belmont will give you 3-ounce tastings for $2, and this price is really worth it, especially given that the alcohol content of these beers is high. Sour beers are not for everyone, but before you make that decision, you must try some of these for yourself. Free your minds, people! While we love it on a hot afternoon after working in the yard, there's more to life than PBR!

Hair of the Dog Brewery and Tasting Room

61 SE Yamhill St.
(503) 232-6585
www.hairofthedog.com

Beer aficionados might be surprised to find Hair of the Dog listed in a chapter about bargain drinking in Portland, for this beer-nerd favorite is notoriously expensive. It's a brewer's brewery, with beers named after the local gods—for example, Fred Eckhardt, who some credit with single-handedly reviving the ancient art of craft brewing in Portland, or Greg Higgins, who is responsible for truly bringing the local and seasonal ethos to Portland restaurants. But the whole point of this book is to show you how to live well for less, and for that reason, you should taste some beer at Hair of the Dog. You can get the "Walk the Dog" sampler of four 3-ounce pours, or you can try individual 3-ounce pours for $2. They often sell on tap things that are next to impossible to buy bottled (or on draft, for that matter). So even if you are paying $6.50 for 12 ounces of something rare, you would be paying twice that for a bottle of it. The tasting room also serves delicious food that usually tops out less than $10 per plate, so there's good value there too.

Mactarnahan's Taproom
2730 NW 31st Ave.
(503) 228-5269
www.macsbeer.com

This Portland stalwart is housed in a beautiful building in an industrial area and is great for group beer tasting in their large restaurant— on Monday night, they have pitchers for $10, and $2 pints on Wednesday. On Saturday, they have samplers plus an appetizer for $15 ($20 for 2 samplers and the appetizer). And on Sunday, children eat for free. But probably the best deal is the Thursday growler special: Fill one, and fill another one for free. (For you non-beer-nerds, growlers are 64-ounce jugs that you can fill up and carry home.)

BEER **FESTIVALS**

Cheers to Belgian Beers
Location varies
http://oregonbeer.org/pctbb

The Catch: Admission is free, but if you want to drink anything, the fee is $15; this gets you your own personal tasting glass and 5 drink tickets. Extra tastes are $1.

Portland's Cheers to Belgian Beers event is held toward the end of April and features—not surprisingly—Belgian-style beers, many of which were even produced with the same yeast strain. This is a contest as well as a festival. Whoever wins the people's choice award gets to select next year's yeast strain, which I guess in the beer world is like having home court advantage. When you experience the variety of beers made under these conditions, you will be surprised. Food carts will be there to sell you food to help you absorb the alcohol, which is fat soluble, so go for something hearty.

Portland International Beerfest
Location varies
www.seattlebeerfest.com/Index2%20PIB.htm

The Catch: There's a $25 entry fee, but you can purchase these for $20 if you buy in advance. Entry fee gets you 10 beer tickets and a tasting glass. Additional tickets are $1; beers cost 1 to 6 tickets. Servings are 4 ounces. Now you know what you are getting into.

This prefunction for the Oregon Brewers Festival—it usually happens during the second weekend in July—features 150 beers from 15 different countries, and is something of a raucous event. There are lots of $1 beers, but to get the best deal, purchase tickets in advance, which not only saves you money but also gets you in faster, and purchase your beers in the Grande Beer Garden, where you can stop messing around with 4-ounce servings and just drink a full pint for $3 or 3 tickets. No kids, but dogs are welcome, and be sure to bring your ID.

Oregon Brewers Festival
Tom McCall Waterfront Park
(503) 778-5917
www.oregonbrewfest.com

In a town that's in love with beer, the Oregon Brewers Festival is like a large, boisterous wedding. Every July, nearly 80,000 people converge upon Portland's waterfront to sample excellent beers and ales from the region as well as those from elsewhere. Eighty brewers from across the continent who specialize in handcrafted beers attend this festival to demonstrate their artistry and win new converts to the fine and ancient art of brewing. You will find every style of beer, from stouts to wheat beers to fruit ales to porters, but each brewery is allowed to showcase only one product. Craft-brewed root beer and other sodas, as well as various alternative beverages, are also featured in a special "Root Beer Garden" for minors and designated drivers. Portland being what it is, you'll also find superb food, as well as great entertainment.

The Oregon Brewers Festival is family friendly, but it does celebrate alcohol, so bear that in mind when planning. It's a good idea to use public transportation or appoint a driver; the festival will not tolerate those who are over-served, so behave. Sometimes it's hot in July—bring water and sunscreen. Admission is free, but visitors must purchase a tasting mug for $6, in addition to wooden tokens for $1 apiece. A tasting pour is $1 (that is, one token), while a full pour is $4 (that is, 4 tokens). Tokens are the currency of the Brewers Festival, so be sure to purchase an adequate amount. The festival runs Thurs through Sun of the last full weekend in July.

Zwickelmania
http://oregonbeer.org/zwickelmania

Zwickelmania is a free event sponsored by the Oregon Brewers Guild in which participants can tour breweries (small and large) and learn about the incredible bounty that is Oregon beer. It happens all over the state on President's Day weekend, but many of the breweries are in Portland. Designate a driver, download a map, and head out. Bring some cash for food—many of the breweries will sell sausages and other beer-friendly cuisine, which you will need.

It's Five O'Clock Somewhere

In food-obsessed Portland, happy hour is often about the menu—which we cover in the Food chapter—on the theory that if the establishment lures you in with cheap and delicious food, you won't mind paying for drinks, which are much more profitable for bar owners. But on any day of the week, you can find somewhere that offers $1 pints if you wear a Hawaiian shirt or $1 well shots just for the heck of it. You just need to know where to look. If your pockets are light, try looking up happy hours using the happy hour finder from the Portland-based online magazine *Barfly* (www.barflymag.com/happy-hour). This handy tool allows you to look up happy hours for right this minute or to plan for the future—just click on the time (including "Now"), the day of the week, and area of town. You can also filter for qualities such as kid-friendly establishments or those that specialize in wine. Try it and you will have an amazingly comprehensive list at your fingertips.

BREWERY **TOURS**

Widmer Brothers Brewing Company
929 N. Russell St.
(503) 281-2437 for beer tour reservations
www.widmer.com

Widmer is one of the earliest of Oregon microbrewers, and they offer free tours of their cool brewery in North Portland. And you will get to sample many of their refreshing beers. You must make a reservation, and you'll need to be 21 or older. Tour times are Fri at 3 p.m. and Sat at 11 a.m. and 12:30 p.m. They ask that you wear close-toed shoes.

DISTILLERY **TOURS**

In keeping with its ethos that absolutely everything is better when it's made at home, Portland has a bourgeoning distillery industry. Most of these new entities are in Southeast Portland, along what is becoming known as **Distillery Row** (www.distilleryrowpdx.com). Six distilleries produce their micro-spirits in a 20-block range, making it possible to sober up between houses if you are walking, which I hope you are. Starting in the spring of 2011, a Distillery Row "Passport" will be available; it combines tasting tours of the distilleries with discounts to nearby restaurants, cafes, and other attractions. There are also package deals at the Juniper Hotel and via Portland Pedicab, but these are not as cheap—though paying someone to bike you around Distillery Row may be one of those investments worth making.

Integrity Spirits (909 SE Yamhill St., 503-729-9794), **New Deal Distilling** (1311 SE 9th Ave., 503-234-2513), and **Deco Distilling** (1512 SE 7th Ave., 503-231-7688) all have tasting hours on Saturday and at a few other times, and it's possible to arrange a tour ahead of time (or see them in the context of a package deal; see the Distillery Row website above). Highball Spirits, specializing in high-end vodka flavored with organic ingredients, does not at press time have retail or tour hours. The following two have organized, regular tours:

House Spirits

2025 SE 7th Ave.
(503) 235-3174
www.housespirits.com

House Spirits produces a variety of alcohols, including Medoyeff Vodka, Aviation Gin, Krogstad Aquavit, and the Apothecary line, which comprises small batch spirits that vary in their content. They are open Tues through Fri from noon to 6 p.m., and their tours are on the hour on Sat. Check the website if you want to be sure that the tours are really happening.

Stone Barn Brandyworks

3315 SE 19th, Ste. B
(503) 775-6747
www.stonebarnbrandyworks.com

Stone Barn specializes in German-style fruit brandies and other liqueurs, including Red Wing Coffee Liqueur, Hard Eight Unoaked Rye Whiskey, pear and apple brandies, Star Crimson Pear Liqueur, Golden Quince Liqueur, and Pinot Noir Oaked Grappa—and that is just for starters. Tours are offered Sat and Sun from 1 to 5:30 p.m.

TRANSPORTATION:
ON THE ROAD AGAIN

*"Everywhere is within walking distance
if you have the time."*

—STEVEN WRIGHT

Portland is a city in which it is possible to live cheaply and well without actually owning a car. I am not saying you should do this—people get very sensitive about this issue—I am merely saying it is possible. You don't have to live without a car. For many reasons, it might be cheaper to hang onto your 1992 Voyager. Or maybe you just like driving. That's fine! But in Portland, you can live without a car if you want to. How is it possible? Part of the reason is municipal infrastructure. The region has emphasized alternative transportation and has dedicated funds to build it. Part of the reason is that Portland is organized around neighborhoods, so many services are often found within walking or biking distance. And part of the reason is that there are a lot of other people sharing cars, riding bikes, and taking the MAX train, so there's social momentum behind it. If you choose to live a low- or no-car lifestyle, you will be in good company.

PUBLIC **TRANSPORTATION**

TriMet
(503) 238-RIDE (trip information)
www.trimet.org

TriMet is the Portland metropolitan area's tri-county transit system, and mastering that system is critical for any low-car lifestyle. It includes the bus, light-rail, and emergent commuter rail systems, and integrates the city-run streetcar line as well. It is extensively networked into the suburbs, so the cheap who live in Wilsonville and Beaverton also benefit from TriMet. The principal attribute for the cheap, however, is the Fareless Square downtown. This region bordered by the Willamette River, Northwest Irving Street, and I-405, provides free rides on buses, MAX light-rail trains, and streetcars within its boundaries and along the transit mall.

The hub of the MAX system is downtown Portland along the major streets that constitute the transit mall. From there, it extends from eastern Multnomah County west to Hillsboro in Washington County, and south to Clackamas. Trains run about every 15 minutes during the day, and there are 4 lines: the Blue Line runs east and west between Gresham and Hillsboro, passing through downtown Portland; the Red Line runs from the Beaverton Transit Center through downtown to the airport; the Yellow Line travels north and south between downtown and the Expo Center, along Interstate Avenue; and the Green Line runs from Portland State University east to Clackamas Town Center. The commuter train service—called WES (Westside Express Service)—connects the southern suburbs of Wilsonville, Tigard, Tualatin, and Beaverton with downtown Portland. It runs on weekday mornings and afternoons, leaving about every half hour.

TriMet fares are based on a zone system and cover buses, MAX trains, and streetcars. A 1- or 2-zone ticket, good for 2 hours, will set you back $2.05, while an all-zone ticket costs $2.35. (Fares are discounted for seniors, students, and children younger than 6.) One special note for the cheap: Bus drivers will not give you change. The best deal, however, is a monthly pass for $92. These passes are widely available (the TriMet website has a comprehensive list of outlets). Better yet, many Portland employers, especially those downtown, where parking is scarce and thus expensive, subsidize TriMet passes for their employees. This is a really good deal, since you can use your pass all over the city, all day, and all night.

Even the cheap hate waiting for the bus. One of the things that makes the TriMet system efficient, and therefore bearable and of value, is its extensive tracking resources (www.trimet.org/transittracker/about.htm). This tool provides real-time information about bus and train arrival times. You can call the system, or look it up online or on your smartphone, and enter your Stop ID number (usually on the sign demarking the bus stop, but also easily available on the TriMet website) to learn when your bus is scheduled to arrive. That way, you can stay inside where it's warm instead of standing outside in the rain wondering when the darn bus is going to get there.

C-Tran
(360) 695-0123, (503) 283-8054
www.c-tran.com

Some cheap bastards live in Vancouver, Washington (aka "The Couv"), and commute across the Columbia River every day. If this is you, you may wish to take advantage of their bus service across the Columbia River to downtown Portland and other select destinations (e.g., Oregon Health & Science University). Commuting from Vancouver to Portland on the Portland Express Service costs $3.25 one way. C-Tran and TriMet honor one another's tickets, so an All-Zone ticket for TriMet can be used on C-Tran. The Monthly Pass cost for the Express is $110.

Streetcars

The Catch: Streetcars are beautiful, clean, cheap, and slow. Bring something to read.

Portland's streetcars have ignited a national revival. They are indisputably a pleasant way to travel, especially if you are not in a hurry. Streetcars travel from the South Waterfront district on the Willamette, through Portland State University north to Good Samaritan Hospital (between NW Lovejoy and NW Northrup at NW 23rd). They follow 10th and 11th Avenues through downtown and the Pearl District, stopping at Powell's City of Books. The city is busy building streetcar service on the east side of the Willamette; the line is expected to open during the fall of 2011.

Streetcars stop every 2 to 3 blocks, and they run from 5:30 a.m. to 11 p.m. Mon through Thurs and until 11:45 p.m. on Fri. Weekend hours are Sat from 7:15 a.m. to 11:45 p.m. and Sun from 7:15 a.m. to 10:30 p.m. Cars arrive every 12 to 15 minutes during peak hours and a bit less frequently at other times. Well-marked, glass-covered streetcar stops, however, are equipped with electronic screens that helpfully note when the next streetcar will arrive.

CAR **SHARING**

Owning a car is a major expense—buying the car, insuring the car, fueling the car, detailing the car, repairing the car: Let's face it, the care and feeding of the car is one of life's major expenses.

But here is one secret to living cheaply and well in Portland, Oregon: You don't need a car. And even if you want a car, you don't need lots of cars, or even one car for every driver. You have many options. You can ride your bike. You can take a sleek streetcar. You can walk. You can live a no- or low-car lifestyle, leaving you a lot more cash for travel, restaurants, or just the rent.

And yet cars are incredibly useful. The frugalisti sometimes need to go to Costco or IKEA, and it's difficult to lug home flat-fold furniture and giant boxes of dish detergent on public transportation. It's cheaper for the whole family to drive to Seattle than for everyone to take the train. Sometimes you really need a car. But why buy a car when you can borrow one?

Zipcar
(503) 328-3539
www.zipcar.com

The Catch: *No smoking, no pets in any cars, ever. Plus steep late fees! So read the fine print before you sign up, and make sure it's for you.*

Zipcar is a car-sharing cooperative that is well established in Portland— unsurprisingly, Portland was a very early adopter of the car-sharing model. Zipcar distributes the costs of owning a car among members—you are charged for the number of hours you use the cars, and after a certain point, for the number of miles you drive. Fees go to cover insurance, gas, mainte- nance, repair, and cleaning. Zipcars are well placed across inner Portland—it is a very popular program—at sites reserved just for Zipcars. (In fact, if you are visiting Portland, don't park in the Zipcar spots! They are well marked with signs, so pay attention. It's not cheap to get a ticket!) Zipcar offers a wide variety of vehicles; many Priuses (of course), but also trucks, minivans, and even cute Mini Coopers. To use a car, you call ahead to make a reser- vation, pick up the car at the designated spot, and return it to the same location at the time you have arranged. You can choose based on the type of vehicle you want or the location you want or both. Gas cards come with the car in case you need to fill up. Zipcar has different levels of membership and a helpful flow chart to help you figure out the appropriate one for you. You can rent cars for a couple of hours or take road trips—as long as you reserve properly.

Peer-to-Peer Car Sharing
Why should your Lamborghini Reventon sit idle in the garage while you are at work all day? The truly cheap would want to maximize opportunity, and beginning in 2012, a new law allows you to do just that: Peer-to-peer car sharing is legal in Oregon. This law simplifies insurance regulations to allow you to rent out your car to your neighbor, and vice versa. Previously, if you borrowed a car from a friend and you were in an accident, he or she was liable for the damages and could even risk cancellation of the policy. The

new law, however, sets up a system for short-term insurance that protects both the car owner and the car borrower. Peer-to-peer car sharing essentially works like Zipcar, but you are borrowing from private citizens rather than a company. **Portland Afoot** (www.portlandafoot.org) is keeping tabs on this new service as it develops, with a page of resources and information.

WALKING

Portland is a city of neighborhoods, and most of these, especially those close to the downtown core, have neighborhood centers with cute restaurants, shops, grocery and drugstores, banks, libraries, schools, dry cleaners, veterinarians, and all the other services required for daily living. It is thus theoretically possible to have a job right by where you live.

If walking is your primary mode of transportation, be sure to choose your neighborhood carefully—you'll want to make sure that there are enough public transportation services to complement your walking lifestyle. Some neighborhoods are well served by multiple bus lines, plus the streetcar or the MAX. Others are not.

Portland has multiple resources dedicated to helping its citizens immerse themselves in their city by walking in it. Start with the City of Portland's transportation office (www.portlandonline.com/transportation), which offers free walking maps (in Spanish too) and provides other important information. **Portland Afoot** (www.portlandafoot.org) is a local nonprofit that publishes a great "10-minute newsmagazine" dedicated to walking, as well as to biking and transiting, throughout the Metro region. This really useful organization also has a newsy blog that provides information on community events, planning sessions, safety data, and other important things. Another nonprofit, **Portland Transport** (www.portlandtransport.com), keeps everyone up to date on transportation policy and practice throughout the region—they keep tabs on legislation and serve as a community hub.

BIKING

Every other month, some publication or another is announcing that Portland is Bicycle City, USA—a reputation that has now gone international. Indeed, the *New York Times*, observing the influx of bicycles into the City of London, wondered whether London is becoming the new Portland. Now this impression has been backed by evidence: According to a 2011 study by researchers from Rutgers University and Virginia Tech, Portland's citizens really do bike more than people in any other city in the US. In spite of hilly terrain and wet weather, we ride bikes persistently and passionately. The study showed that 15 percent of Portlanders don't own a car, and many of those are biking households—in fact, 18 percent of Portland households use a bike as either their primary or secondary mode of transportation. Between 1990 and 2009, Portland increased its "bike mode share" from 1.1 to 5.8 percent, the highest in the nation. For some contrast, New York City's bike mode share is 0.6 percent, even though New York and Portland have about the same number of bike path miles. Bike commuting to downtown Portland almost tripled during the period between 2000 and 2008, from 3 percent to more than 8 percent—or put another way, there were 178 percent more bike trips in 2008. And some neighborhoods are home to even more enthusiastic bikers—the inner Northeast and inner Southeast Portland neighborhoods have 13 percent bike share, a fact that will surprise no one trying to drive downtown from these neighborhoods on a weekday morning.

One of the reasons for the explosive growth of biking in Portland is the city's fertile bike culture—more than 4,000 rides and events annually, including a bike show at the Oregon Convention Center in early April—and robust infrastructure to support it. This includes bike lanes and paths, traffic routes that have been "calmed" with speed bumps and traffic circles, bike route signage, ample bike parking, employer bike incentives, and integration with public transportation. In fact, 100 percent of Portland's buses have bike racks on the front, meaning that you can use both modes of transportation. And you can take your bike on the MAX light rail and the streetcar as well. Does that mean that Portland is free from crazy, nonhelmeted bikers who shred through traffic? No—human nature being what it is. But they are in the minority. Most bikers are peacefully minding their own business and obeying the traffic laws, following the well-marked bike routes. In short, then, should you decide to embrace the biking lifestyle, you will have plenty of support.

One notable event is **Pedalpalooza** (www.shift2bikes.org/pedalpalooza/index.shtml), an annual festival held each June that is a citywide celebration of all things bicycle-related. There are many free things to do, from yoga for bikers to special biking brewery tours, and most of these events are created and organized by local groups or even simply by inspired individuals. It is an organic and idiosyncratic—practically anarchic—two weeks of events. Of special note is the World Naked Bike Ride, which brings together thousands of riders, and even more spectators, who in all their glory thread their way through Portland's streets in protest of fossil fuels and in support of the vulnerability of cyclists. (There is also a "World Clothed Bike Ride" for those who find the thought of bike seat-skin contact more uncomfortable than revolutionary). Clothed or not, you will need bike gear, and you can find more about where to find it cheaply in the Shopping chapter.

BIKING **RESOURCES**

Portland Transportation Office
www.portlandonline.com/transportation

Portland's city-sponsored bicycle office, which has a comprehensive Bicycle Master Plan, is a regional treasure. It has established a network of bike paths and routes that spans nearly 200 miles, including dedicated paths and on-street bike lanes. They have posted signs all over town that tell cyclists how far, and in which direction, their destinations are. They will tell you how to ride your bike from the airport to downtown. They have studied traffic patterns and established bike safety green zones at major intersections to help keep bikers injury-free. They will help you find a bike locker. But the cheap among us will especially love it for their free resources: This office provides online and downloadable maps and other information about bike routes, bike parking, safety, and commuting—including fantastic maps of 7 fabulous rides around the city of Portland.

Bicycle Transportation Alliance (BTA)
(503) 226-0676
www.bta4bikes.org

One pillar of support is the Bicycle Transportation Alliance, established in 1990. The BTA is an advocacy group that works to promote the infrastructure necessary to promote safe and extensive biking. They have been instrumental in helping the city plan for more bike lanes as well as helping employers figure out how to encourage bike commuting and businesses to help figure out bike parking. They persuaded TriMet to allow bikes on buses and to make sure the bridges that cross the Willamette are safe for bikes. BTA also works with local promoters to make sure festivals and events have ample bike parking. They train schoolchildren to ride safely. They sponsor biking events such as the Portland Bridge Pedal. And they maintain lists and links of very useful things for bikers on their excellent website.

As an aside, BTA and the city's support of biking has led to a small boom in local bike-related businesses. These include bike transportation planners; innovative designers of gear, helmets, and customized bikes; biking plumbers; biking coffee roasters; biking gardeners; and many more services that are very Portland.

Bike Portland
www.bikeportland.org

One of the best sources of bike information is Bike Portland, a blog dedicated to bike news, policy, and analysis. One of their outstanding services is maintaining a registry of stolen bikes, and they also help you figure out how to get your bike back. But they also provide updates on local biking news stories, point out new shops and services, profile events, alert readers to bike lane closures and traffic diversions, and generally provide authoritative information about anything related to bikes in Portland. This is a must-read for anyone interested in a biking lifestyle in the area. Add it to your RSS feed.

BIKE **REPAIR**

Portland has many, many, many bike shops. Some of these are listed in the Shopping chapter. Some of these also do bike repair. Below are several that we have found to have outstanding service and value.

One tip, speaking of repairs: Keep bus fare on you in case you get a flat tire or a spoke goes out or you need some other repair on your way to work—you can throw your bike on the bus, get to your meeting on time, and deal with your flat tire later.

Bicycle Repair Collective
4438 SE Belmont St.
(503) 233-0564
www.bicyclerepaircol.net

This is a favorite shop. I will confess that while I ride my bike a lot, I hate to maintain it. So I choose the non-cheap option of having the amazing bike mechanics at the Bicycle Repair Collective fix my bike for me. The last time I got it back, it rode better than the day I bought it. It was beautiful. Plus they are really nice and not bike snobs, which is important for cheap people. If you are cheaper than I am, the Bicycle Repair Collective is also a great option—you can rent their workspace and do all the repairs yourself and use their tools for $10 per hour.

Community Cycling Center
1700 NE Alberta St.
(503) 287-8786
www.communitycyclingcenter.org

The Community Cycling Center is a great resource in Northeast Portland that not only has a bike shop and repair facility but also has excellent classes that teach bike maintenance and other tips. These classes are dedicated to different interests or audiences—there are classes for women, classes for commuters, and so on—and they also focus on teaching bike safety to kids. Another great service they provide is free bike lights, which is terribly important in a biking city.

Kerr Repair Kiosk
North side of the Hawthorne Bridge at Salmon Springs

The Kerr Repair Kiosk is a feature of a local bike rental shop in Waterfront Park. They have a little spot for repairing your bike if you are downtown and get a flat or have another issue. You have to do the work yourself though.

HEADING **OUT** OF **TOWN**

Amtrak
Union Station
800 NW 6th Ave.
(503) 273-4865 (station information)
(503) 273-4866 (daily arrival and departure information)
(800) 872-7245 (reservations and schedule information)
www.amtrakcascades.com

The Catch: Those younger than 16 can't take the Amtrak bus without an adult.

The train service in the Pacific Northwest is not nearly as robust as it is in the Northeast Corridor, but it is nevertheless a great way to get to Seattle or Vancouver, BC. The trip to Seattle takes a little over 3 hours and the train drops you off right by Safeco Field, so Portlanders love to take the train up to watch the Mariners, spend the night in Seattle, and head back in the morning. Since driving to Seattle from Portland is its own special hell once you reach Olympia, the train is a lovely alternative—you can read, look at Puget Sound, have a glass of wine. But it is not always cheap! Round-trip tickets start at about $30, so it is less expensive for me to drive my family even with gas prices the way they are today. If you are on your own, however, it might actually be cheaper to take the train.

Amtrak has other services that, while also not cheap, can support your low-car lifestyle and are still cheaper than owning or renting a car. For example, they offer bus service to Cannon Beach, Astoria, and other coastal destinations for $34 round trip and $17 one way. The bus runs several times a day and it is clean and pleasant. This is a great alternative for the low-car

> # Getting to the Airport
> You could take a taxi for $35, or you could take the **MAX Red Line** for $2.35. It takes about 40 minutes from downtown—on weekday evenings, it can be much faster than driving, especially if you factor in parking in the airport's economy lot (the preferred lot of cheap bastards everywhere) and boarding the shuttle. Trains arrive at PDX, Portland's airport, beginning at 4:44 a.m. (4:45 on the weekends). The final train departs PDX at 11:49 p.m. every day.

household. For example, if you're staying at the beach but must arrive at different times, send the teenagers ahead to the campsite to set up, while you finish work and then relax on the bus, and have them pick you up later.

Craigslist Rideshare
www.portland.craigslist.org

Ridesharing requests and offers on the Portland site largely concentrate on the I-5 corridor: Seattle, San Francisco, and Eugene, though you can also secure cross-country rideshares as well. Craigslist is also useful for rides to the coast and to Mt. Hood for a $5 gas contribution. Use your street smarts when riding with strangers, please.

CHILD'S PLAY:
CHEAP ACTIVITIES

"Do not, on a rainy day, ask your child what he feels like doing, because I assure you that what he feels like doing, you won't feel like watching."

—FRAN LEBOWITZ

One of the best things about Portland is its attention to the pleasures of daily living. We aren't New York or Paris—we don't have free days at the Louvre. We do have a city that is fun to explore for children, with lots of plazas, playgrounds, and fountains, as well as farmers' markets, fairs, gardens, museums, and other things that entice children. We also embrace our public schools and public parks, enriching life for all. Indeed, one of the ways to live cheaply in the Portland Metro area is to join the 90 percent of families who send their children to public schools—schools that have outstanding features such as the International Baccalaureate program or language immersion programs.

For these and many other reasons, Portland is a great family city—whether you are visiting or living here. This chapter covers many of the kid-specific activities and attractions available in the area. But many of the other chapters in this book have good tips that are child- or family-appropriate, so be sure to look there too.

GREAT **PLAYGROUNDS,** PARKS & **WALKS**

As noted throughout this book, we love our parks in Portland, and these beloved public institutions are found throughout the city—whether they are sweet, tiny pocket parks such as Piccolo Park (SE 27th Avenue and Division) or expansive domains such as Washington Park (see below). The city's parks office, Portland Parks & Recreation, has an excellent website (www .portlandparks.org), and one of its features is a "park finder" that allows you to search for a park that has the features you are seeking—water spray areas, playgrounds, tennis courts, or anything else. This useful service can help you plan birthday parties or other events: www.portlandonline.com/parks/finder. Below are some of our favorite playgrounds and parks.

Gabriel Park
SW 45th Avenue and Vermont Street

Gabriel Park—which is also the home of the Southwest Community Center, complete with fabulous pools and fitness facilities—is also a great outdoor park. Its rolling, grassy hills are perfect for exhausting high-energy children before dinner. There's a good play structure—and there's a good skate park for older kids.

Grant Park
NE 33rd Avenue and US Grant Place

Grant Park is a beautiful 20-acre park in Northeast Portland; it surrounds Grant High School, and it is the setting for many events in the novels of Beverly Cleary, who grew up in the neighborhood. Thus, in addition to the pool, playground, and paths, there is the Beverly Cleary Sculpture Garden, where you can visit Ramona Quimby, Ribsy, and Henry Huggins.

Irving Park
NE 7th Avenue and Fremont

Pretty Irving Park in Northeast Portland has a nice playground and excellent sports courts—tennis, basketball, and volleyball—as well as plenty of room for soccer and baseball. Years ago, before it was a park, it was a racetrack. Maybe the kids are picking up lingering frenetic energy from that.

Jamison Square
NW 11th and NW Johnson

Jamison Square is a beautiful piazza in the Pearl District—it is surrounded by leafy trees and cafes on the perimeter and landscaped with golden decomposed granite and brick, stone, and wood. It is often filled with people playing boules and this is where Portland's Bastille Day celebration is held. It is also one of the most popular places to take small children because it has a large fountain designed for playing: The water advances and retreats, beckoning hot children on sweltering days.

Laurelhurst Park
SE Cesar E Chavez Boulevard (SE 39th) and Stark Street

Laurelhurst Park has a fine playground, a small lake, and inviting paths, along with the usual park amenities (picnic tables, basketball, etc.). Laurelhurst is notable for a couple of other reasons besides its playground: It is the site of Portland Parks & Recreation's dance studio, housed in a pretty building built in 1915, and it was designed by a planner who had been trained by the Olmsted brothers, who designed Central Park in New York (as well as Washington Park here in Portland). Laurelhurst used to be the site of the coronation of the Rose Festival Queen, which took place on rafts floating on the lake. Alas, the duck and catfish overpopulation prevents such picturesque festivities now. But it is still a fun park for children and adults, despite the lack of pageantry.

Mt. Tabor Park
SE 60th and Salmon Street

Lovely Mt. Tabor Park has the distinction of being sited on one of the two dormant volcanoes within city limits in the US (the other is in Bend, Oregon). This wonderful park has views of other volcanoes—Mt. St. Helens (not so dormant) and Mt. Hood, as well as beautiful paths through tall forests, reservoirs with attractive crenellated walls, and an excellent play structure.

Washington Park
Top of SW Park Place

The best playground in Portland is probably the one at Washington Park—the well-designed, large facility, near the Rose Garden, will keep small children and their older siblings very busy running, climbing, sliding, and swinging on the bright equipment. The park, which also hosts the Oregon Zoo, the Hoyt Arboretum, and the International Rose Test Garden, will provide hours, even days, of things to do.

FARMS & FAIRS

Portland Farmers' Market
Portland State University
1800 SW Broadway at Montgomery
(503) 241-0032
www.portlandfarmersmarket.org

The Catch: While going to the Farmers' Market is free, leaving from the Farmers' Market without spending money will be a challenge. But at least you get locally grown, organic, sustainable food out of it!

As noted in the Food chapter, the Portland Farmers' Market is a multigenerational weekly festival, with lots of live music, multiple harvest festivals, cooking demonstrations, the balloon man (who will make any kind of balloon shape in the color of your choice for a small fee!), samples, cooking classes for kids, and generalized conviviality even in the pouring rain. Traditions include dancing at the live music stage after breakfast from Pine State Biscuits or one of the many local bakeries that sell at the market, accompanied by hot chocolate and coffee. This is a family favorite, since it is completely free, very festive, educational, and fun. It is held Mar through Dec, Sat 8 a.m. to 2 p.m.

Fir Point Farms
14601 Arndt Rd., Aurora
(503) 678-2455
http://firpointfarms.com

The Catch: City slickers who want to feed the goats pay 25 cents, and some rides and games cost extra.

About half an hour's drive from downtown Portland, Fir Point Farms is a favorite destination for families with bored children. They have a wonderful harvest festival, but they also have pony rides and the chickens, turkeys, cows, horses, and goats throughout the year. Feeding the goats is really fun; the goats are often in tree houses, and you can send food up to them in little buckets that are on a pulley system. Fir Point Farms is open from 9 a.m. to 6 p.m. every day.

Flower Farmer
2512 N. Holly Rd., Canby
(503) 266-3581
www.flowerfarmer.com
www.phoenixandholly.com

The Catch: Riding the train costs $4 for kids younger than 13 and $5 for adults, though admission is free.

The Flower Farmer is a flower and pumpkin-harvest destination that also includes a 15-inch narrow-gauge train that winds through the fields. The train circles the farm, past displays and through tunnels, stopping at a petting zoo with chickens, turkeys, and a miniature donkey, as well as a large hay pyramid, depending on the time of year. It winds around to the gift shop, where you can purchase ice cream, produce, and dried and fresh flowers. The train is seasonal—check the website or call ahead to make sure it's running.

The Canby Ferry

The Canby Ferry is an old-fashioned river ferry that has been taking people and vehicles across the Willamette since 1914. Before the Willamette's many bridges were built, everyone used to cross the river by ferry—you can too. It is a fun addition to a trip to Fir Point Farms or the Flower Farmer. To get there from the Flower Farmer, follow Holly Road north to the end, where you'll reach the ferry. The ferry holds 9 vehicles and takes about 5 minutes to cross. There is a small charge for cars ($2); bikes and pedestrians ride free. The Canby Ferry runs from 6:45 a.m. to 9:15 p.m. daily (www.co.clackamas.or.us /transportation/transit/ferry.htm; the website has directions and other helpful information as well).

The Pumpkin Patch
16511 NW Gillihan Rd., Sauvie Island
(503) 621-3874
www.thepumpkinpatch.com

The Pumpkin Patch is a very popular local farm that probably every child in Portland has visited at least once through school field trips, but it never seems to get old and it appeals to all ages. There's a u-pick berry field as well as other produce for sale. They also create a very elaborate corn maze every year (they call it the "Maize") that attracts teenagers and adults from all around. It's free to visit, and there are many no-cost activities such as hayrides, but some things, such as the corn maze, cost extra. To get to the Pumpkin Patch, take US 30 west to Sauvie Island and circle left under the bridge. This will place you on Gillihan Road, and you'll find the farm after about 2 miles—watch for the signs.

ARCADE **GAMES**

Electric Castles Wunderland
3451 SE Belmont St.
(503) 238-1617
www.wunderlandgames.com

Spending bottle deposits on arcade games is a very Portland economic exchange. Wunderland carries all the latest video and pinball games, including test games, and new arrivals are common. This is a great spot for birthday parties for older kids. There is a small admission fee, but most games run on nickels. The Avalon and Milwaukie Wunderland locations also show family-friendly, first-run movies at very good prices—usually less than $3

Outdoor & Indoor Games at Portland Parks & Recreation

One of the best values for families in Portland is the extensive sports programming run by the Portland Parks & Recreation department. The team sports and individual lessons are far more affordable through the parks programs compared with the other local leagues and may be more appropriate for many children, and these activities are thus highly regarded by Portlanders. Activities range from swimming lessons to yoga to organized leagues for competitive basketball, tennis, volleyball, soccer, baseball, cross-country running, and track and field. Not only that, however, but they also have extensive fitness facilities for use by the whole family. Even activities such as roller skating are offered—the cheapest roller skating in town is at the Mount Scott Community Center (5530 SE 72nd Ave.; 503-823-3183)—it costs $3; $1 for skate rental.

Class sessions for all activities are offered continually. More about these facilities can be found on their well-organized website (www.portlandparks.org), and a full list of area facilities is found in Appendix B.

($4 for starred attractions). Additional locations are at 10306 NE Halsey St. (503-255-7333); 11011 SE Main St., Milwaukie (503-653-2222); and 4070 Cedar Hills Blvd., Beaverton (503-626-1665).

Ground Kontrol Classic Arcade
511 NW Couch St.
(503) 796-9364
www.groundkontrol.com

Ground Kontrol features 90 vintage arcade games from the 1970s through the 1990s—a really good activity when the rains are no longer bearable in April. Or May. Or June. It's all-ages until 5 p.m., then 21 and over after that. Bring your ID. Most video and pinball games cost 1 or 2 quarters.

SKATEBOARDING

Burnside Skate Park
Under the Burnside Bridge on the east side of the Willamette River

The Burnside Skate Park was born out of the desire of skateboarders to have somewhere to go where they wouldn't be ticketed. They hand-built this park, and when the city saw what they had done, and realized that the city would be better off with a skate park than to risk public structures every-where to the wheels of skateboards, they saw that it was good. If your kids are new to skateboarding, try to go early in the day, at off-peak times. This park is free. You need to wear a helmet. Portland is one of the few cities to have an actual skateboard master plan, and it was inspired by this park.

STORY **TIMES**

Barnes & Noble
Lloyd Center
1317 Lloyd Ave.
(503) 249-0800
www.barnesandnoble.com

Area Barnes & Noble bookstores not only offer books but also have free story times and author events—and not just for preschoolers. Authors who write books for older readers are also featured regularly. The Lloyd Center location

---

Library Story Times

The **Multnomah County Library** system (www.multcolib.org) has a comprehensive story time and reading program for even the youngest readers—they want to hook the little ones early and build their customer base. Librarians and trained staff provide weekly stories, songs, and activities that are age- and culturally appropriate.

Book Babies is for babies to age 12 months and makes babies happy because it is filled with songs and rhymes, as well as books and other babies. Tiny Tots is geared to 1-year-olds, and Toddler Storytime to 2-year-olds; these focus on interactive songs, stories, and other activities. Preschool Storytime is targeted to children ages 3 to 6, and Family Storytime lets everyone from birth to 6, along with a parent or other adult, come together to enjoy these activities. In addition, there are some unique story times: a Sensory Storytime for children who have difficulties with sensory integration, a Mandarin-English and a Cantonese-English story time, story time for Spanish speakers, and ones for those who speak Vietnamese and Russian as well.

Finally, the library offers Pajama Time, a story time later in the evening—great for working parents. Days and times for these activities vary with the season, so check your local branch or the web for updated times. A listing of all the Multnomah County libraries and other local libraries is found in Appendix C.

---

is one of our favorites, but there are 6 total in the area, and they all have events, usually on weekday mornings and on Saturday. Another favorite is the Beaverton location, 18300 NW Evergreen Pkwy., Beaverton (503-645-3046).

A Children's Place
4807 NE Fremont St.
(503) 284-8294
www.achildrensplacebookstore.com

This is an independent book and toy store in the Beaumont neighborhood, and they have a nice events selection that includes things targeted for adults. Thursday morning storytelling is the community favorite, but there are others throughout the week, including book groups and music events, and they are all free!

Powell's Books
(503) 228-4651
www.powells.com

The three main Powell's stores—City of Books, 1005 W. Burnside St.; Cedar Hills, 3415 SW Cedar Hills Blvd., Beaverton; and Hawthorne, 3723 SE Hawthorne Blvd.—have a very active series of readings and workshops for children. They have story times for younger readers and author readings for their older siblings, but they also have wonderful free writing workshops with local and national writers. Sometimes the "teachers" are children who have themselves published—it's really fun to listen to these young writers advise their peers. Check the calendar on the website for comprehensive details.

MUSEUMS & **ATTRACTIONS**

ALWAYS FREE

Alpenrose Dairy
6149 SW Shattuck Rd.
(503) 244-1133
www.alpenrose.com

Alpenrose Dairy is a large, sprawling museum and sports complex in South-west Portland that really did once have a dairy—they still produce milk, ice cream, and other dairy products, though the cows are now at other Willamette Valley farms. It now features a Western-style village, as well as the main attraction: the Alpenrose Stadium, which hosts Little League games, including the Little League World Series. You will also find several racing arenas, including a quarter-midget track, a BMX track, and an Olympic-style velodrome—one of only 20 in the US. Alpenrose also hosts a yearly Easter egg hunt. There are no charges to attend Little League and other events, and while they would love it if you purchased concessions, you are also welcome to bring in your own food.

Jeff Morris Fire Museum
Belmont Firehouse
900 SE 35th Ave.
(503) 823-3615
www.jeffmorrisfoundation.org

The Catch: While the museum is free, the hours are not consistent. Your best bet is to call ahead or check the website to plan your visit.

The historic Belmont Firehouse is home to this museum, which educates children and adults about antique fire equipment and other relics of past firefighting approaches. In addition to being able to explore a modern fire truck, children can see an 1863 hand-pumper, an 1870 hand-drawn ladder truck, and an 1870 steam-pumper engine. Best of all is a fire pole to practice sliding down. The museum is named after firefighter Jeff Morris, who established the safety-education program at the Portland Fire Bureau. There are also Saturday open houses held throughout the year.

Kidd's Toy Museum
1300 SE Grand Ave. at Main Street
(503) 233-7807
http://kiddstoymuseum.com

Frank Kidd was an automotive parts businessman who began to collect cars and other transportation-related toys such as planes and trains to amuse himself and his colleagues. But his collection grew as he extended his interests to other kinds of toys, and thus the museum was born to share his rare finds with the public. Visiting this museum is an interesting antidote to the screen-focused toys of today. Note the unusual collection of mechanical banks. Kidd's Toy Museum is free and is open Mon through Thurs from noon until 6 p.m., and on Fri from 1 until 6 p.m. Weekend visits can be arranged by appointment.

3D Center of Art and Photography
1928 NW Lovejoy St.
(503) 227-6667
www.3dcenter.us

The Catch: Children 14 and younger never pay admission fees, but adults pay $5.

Portland has many unique qualities, and one of them is that we are the home of the only museum in the world entirely dedicated to the 3-D experience. The 3D Center for Art & Photography features old-fashioned 3-D technologies such as stereocards and Viewmasters as well as state-of-the-art computer-generated 3-D. There are a number of interactive exhibits, as well as featured artists each month. You can visit the 3D Center Thurs through Sat, from 11 a.m. to 5 p.m., and on Sun from 1 to 5 p.m. Everyone gets in free on the first Thursday of the month, when the museum has extended hours until 9 p.m.

SOMETIMES FREE

Oregon Museum of Science and Industry
1945 SE Water Ave.
(503) 797-4000
www.omsi.edu

The Catch: Parking is not free—it costs $2 per vehicle. The Omnimax, planetarium, and USS Blueback all incur separate charges as well.

OMSI (which for you visitors is pronounced *Ahm-zee*) is a favorite destination for Portland area families, especially during the long, rainy winter. And it's a popular site for field trips. It features permanent and visiting science exhibitions, a planetarium, an earthquake room, an OMNIMAX theater, and laser shows. There is also wonderful play equipment for preschoolers, and for older children, interesting exhibits such as the USS *Blueback*, which is a diesel-powered submarine permanently moored at OMSI. There is a cafeteria and you are welcome to save money by bringing snacks from home and eating them there. OMSI also offers many camps and other education programs, and it is usually open on Monday when Portland public schools are not in session during the school year, in case you are wondering what to do with the kids. OMSI is not cheap, but admission is sharply discounted to $2 on the first Sunday of the month, and children 2 and under are always free.

Portland Children's Museum
4015 SW Canyon Rd.
(503) 223-6500
www.portlandcm.org

The Catch: Parking costs $2. Also, in a bit of role reversal, all adults must be accompanied by children, as a safety measure.

The Portland Children's Museum is conveniently located next to the Oregon Zoo. The museum has activities that appeal to a variety of ages—there are inventive areas for playing store and restaurant; there's a compelling waterworks room, where you can control the rush and flow of water through pipes into pools; there are rooms for dress up, story times, and music. And there is an excellent art studio, with facilities for collages (the "Garage") and great clay facilities, including a kiln. The museum is open Tues through Sun from 9 a.m. to 5 p.m., but they stay open until 8 p.m. on Thurs and on the first Friday of each month. Admission fees are waived at these First Friday events when you attend between 6 and 8 p.m. There is no charge for children younger than 1.

CHEAP

The Oregon Zoo
Washington Park
4001 SW Canyon Rd.
(503) 226-1561
www.oregonzoo.org

The Catch: There are extra fees for the Zoo Railway, some rides, and for parking.

Children and their parents love the Oregon Zoo. It's thrilling to be face to face with an Amur leopard separated only by a fat inch of Plexiglas. It's fun to watch the animals in their native-like habitat. It's exciting to hold a tarantula. It's scary to witness the crocodile. It's intriguing to try to spy the gray wolf. It's compelling to see how many things there are to climb on, how many trails there are to wander down, how soft the grass in the amphitheater is when you are running on it. There are trains, rides, zoo camps, concerts—it is no wonder that we all love the Oregon Zoo. The Oregon Zoo is open every day, except Christmas Day, from 9 a.m. until 4 p.m., except

---

Roadtrip to the A.C. Gilbert Museum

Pretending you are a Maasai herder, a 19th-century explorer, or a modern astronaut are just a few of the compelling activities available at the **A.C. Gilbert Museum** in Salem—a truly worthy excursion from Portland. This museum complex, made up of three Victorian houses on the Willamette, is filled with interactive exhibitions. A. C. Gilbert, a Salem native, was a toy inventor who gave us, among other things, the Erector Set and American Flyer trains. This museum is a fitting tribute to his contribution to American childhood. Hours are Mon through Sat 10 a.m. to 5 p.m. and Sun from noon to 5 p.m. The cheap bastard will buy a family membership, which gives you membership benefits at many of the area museums for a lot less than buying memberships at those other museums. Shhhh. The A.C. Gilbert Museum is at 116 Marion St. NE, Salem (503-371-3631, 800-208-9514; www.acgilbert.org).

---

from May 15 to September 15, when it is open from 8 a.m. until 6 p.m. The zoo stays open for an hour after the gates close, unless you're attending a special event or concert, when you can stay longer. The Zoo Railway has a separate fee. The cheapest way to visit—normally, it's $10.50 for adults and $7.50 for children—is to go on the second Tuesday of each month, when admission is discounted to $4 per person. Children younger than 3 are always admitted for free. You can save $1.50 off the price of admission by presenting your MAX ticket.

World Forestry Center
4033 SW Canyon Rd.
(503) 228-1367
www.worldforestry.org

The Catch: Parking fees will set you back $2.

This museum, next to the Oregon Zoo, is devoted to education about the influence of forests on human experience and in the natural world. It has a number of intriguing permanent exhibitions, many of them on complex matters of sustainability, brought to life with large dioramas (think *A Night at the Museum*). Lest this sound too educational to be fun, there are lots of shiny bits too—for example, a virtual smoke-jumping experience, a virtual white-water rafting experience, and a timberjack harvester simulator. The center also features many special activities, including an annual show featuring Oregon woodworkers and carvers. There is also an art gallery with temporary exhibits. The World Forestry Center Museum is open daily from 10 a.m. to 5 p.m. daily. On Wednesday, admission is discounted to $2 per person (regular prices are $8 for adults and $5 for children).

SHOPPING:
BARGAIN BASEMENT

*"A bargain is something you can't use
at a price you can't resist."*

—FRANKLIN P. JONES

One of the reasons that Portland is a cheap person's paradise is that there is no sales tax in Oregon. (This is actually a mixed blessing when I travel: I can't bring myself to shop in most other cities when I can get the same things at home 8.25 percent more cheaply.) Cutting out the sales tax is only part of the allure, however. Portland has creative entrepreneurs who will sell you cleverly designed sportswear, delicious food, attractive housewares, and other things that you want—at discounted prices if you know where to find them. There are dozens of thrift and resale stores in the area—in DIY Portland, reselling stuff on eBay that you purchased for pennies at the Goodwill Outlet is a second job for about half of the city's population. We also have our share of outlet stores for the times when you want to own something that no one else has owned before. Another alternative is my house: After many years of thrifting and bargain hunting, you could just come to my house and shop there.

People do leave things by the curb with "Free" signs on them, hoping that you will take whatever it is away and spare them a trip to the dump or the Goodwill. We obtained a beautiful slipper chair that way, and I will confess to leaving some things by the curb myself: lawnmowers, boxes of old dresses, odd pieces of stone or wood. One does need to be careful, though. Once my husband was loading our luggage into the car—we were on our way to the airport—and a new neighbor walking by assumed it was being left on the curb and she could take it. It wasn't.

The only thing more fun than scoring a fantastic bargain is telling other people how they can also score fantastic bargains, so let's get started.

TRASH **OR** TREASURE

Craigslist
www.portland.craigslist.org

If you are used to reading *New York Times* articles on how someone furnished their whole apartment with a piquant combination of Eames chairs, Mitchell Gold + Bob Williams sofas, and Heath Ceramics dishes, all bought for a pittance on Craigslist because of an unfortunate divorce—well, such finds are more rare in the Portland area. Yet you can still get great deals. I bought an ice-cream maker for $15 from someone who was leaving for an extended stay in Ireland the next day, and my friend outfitted the backyard of her new house with a beautiful set of teak furniture for $200. The free section has the most pure bargains, of course—useful if you want to get rid of things, but also if you want to score free firewood, chicken coops, bookcases, mattresses, pianos, hot tubs, or any other manner of things that people don't want. The bartering section is fun too.

Eastmoreland Garage Sale

Established in 1985, this event is sometimes tagged "the Northwest's Biggest Garage Sale." It might be true—it involves well over 100 homes in one of Portland's nicest neighborhoods and is a treasure trove of household items, clothing, electronics, games, books, sports equipment, furniture, and everything else you would expect from such an event. It's usually held the last weekend of June, beginning at 8 a.m. on Sat. Experienced yard-salers arrive a little early to get a map (don't bug the homeowners, though—that's rude!), and based on the map, park in a central spot so it's easy to get back to the car without having to schlep your new treasures all over the neighborhood. You should also bring water and lots of bills and quarters.

Freecycle
www.freecycle.org

A major component of a cheap lifestyle is reusing stuff that someone else doesn't want anymore. Freecycle is an online network where people who want to get rid of their stuff offer it up for free for those who would like to take it off their hands. This worldwide network is moderated by volunteers at the local level. Freecycle Portland is, like other Freecycle groups, run out of Yahoo Groups. You don't need a Yahoo account to use it, but it does make life easier if you think you'll be Freecycling a great deal. Freecycle is especially great for home repair and gardening projects, as well as for odd things like if you need a power cord for your old Mac mini. One piece of advice: Unless you are into Extreme Freecycling, set your account so that you just receive the daily digest. Otherwise you will be overwhelmed with e-mails.

CHEAP **FASHION**

Buffalo Exchange
1036 W. Burnside St.
(503) 222-3418

Buffalo Exchange is a west-coast resale chain that specializes in fashionable clothes, shoes, and accessories for men, women, and sometimes children. Look for popular brands and recent styles, as well as long lines at the very picky buying counter. They do carry some nice vintage styles, but most of the clothing is contemporary. Also look for stylish, well-priced shoes, sun-

Frugal Living, Northwest Style

One year I decided to observe "The Compact," a movement in which adherents agree not to purchase anything new for a year. As soon as I made my pledge, I went on eBay and bought 10 dinner plates in my beloved wedding china pattern. (It was the beginning of the recession, and people were cleaning out their storage units.) The irony was not lost on me, however—I recognized that accumulating more things wasn't exactly what the pledge was about. I was trying to live more simply, not simply refusing to buy new things. So I went looking for some kindred souls to help sustain me in my quest for simple and cheaper living. Happily for me, I was not alone. I found a number of online writers documenting similar journeys. Better yet, my companions are based here in the Northwest, making their advice and observations particularly relevant.

One favorite is Katy Wolk-Stanley's **The Nonconsumer Advocate** (http://thenonconsumeradvocate.com). This Portland-based blogger writes about her practice to "use it up, wear it out, make it do, or do without," helping readers practice the old-fashioned virtue of thrift. She is a fan of libraries, bartering, bargains, hanging laundry rather than using the dryer—even in Portland—yard sales, selling things on eBay, baking, gardening, mending, darning, and generally doing things yourself. She relates her tales while having a full-time job

glasses, bags, and other wardrobe necessities. A second location is at 1420 SE 37th Ave. (503-234-1302).

Crossroads Trading Co.

3736 SE Hawthorne Blvd.
(503) 239-8099
www.crossroadstrading.com

Sometimes I think that my daughters' wardrobe consists entirely of things they have bought at and then resold to Crossroads and Buffalo Exchange. Crossroads is a favorite stop in the retail and resale heaven that is Hawthorne. Here you will find popular styles and brands, as well as some vintage and some higher-end items. Prices are a little lower than Buffalo Exchange,

and a family. Far from making readers feel deprived, however, Wolk-Stanley inspires them. The Nonconsumer Advocate styles her frugal and simple lifestyle into an interesting daily adventure, one that has its share of failures as well as successes.

Another blogger is **Modern Thrifter** (http://modernthrifter.com), based in the Seattle area. This writer shares her quest to create a harmonious midcentury-style home on a limited budget. The blog is full of pragmatic advice for repurposing things found at Goodwill, as well as meditations on whether thrifting is a productive habit or an addiction. She shares her tips (re-dye your jeans! Restore vintage veneer!) and her finds (a fantastic modern coffee table for $7!), as well as shopping adventures and musings on family life in these modern times.

Finally, it's worth noting that J.D. Roth, who writes **Get Rich Slowly** (www.getrichslowly.org), lives in the Portland area. His personal finance tips and resources are detailed and comprehensive and have gained such wider readership that he quit his job and devotes himself full time to his blog. Like Wolk-Stanley, his readership is international and comprehensive, but particularly helpful for Northwest readers. Yet in many ways, his advice basically comes down to this: Spend less and don't buy stuff you can't afford. Maybe reading his blog, and this book, can help in that endeavor.

and we have had better luck at the buying counter here than we have had at Buffalo, although I do know people who have had the opposite experience, so you just never know.

Little Edie's Five and Dime
3120 N. Williams Ave.
(503) 284-1051
www.littleediesfiveanddime.com

If you are reading this book, you probably already know that a few items of vintage clothing can really bolster a frugal person's wardrobe, but you may not know that Little Edie's is a good place to find them. This shop in North Portland carries a well-edited collection of vintage clothing, as well as some decor and odds and ends. Little Edie's is noted for its excellent prices, as well as its shoes, dresses, vintage jeans, and nice customer service.

Magpie
520 SW 9th Ave.
(503) 220-0920

Magpie has excellent vintage clothing organized by era—gorgeous clothing, bags, and other accessories. One nice thing about Magpie is that they carry a large selection of men's clothing. This is a vintage shop, not a thrift store, so don't be surprised if you see a suit for $50 or more—but it will be a beautiful suit, well cut in a good fabric, and so of good value. One of the other charms of Magpie is that they have tags that are interesting and informative about the garment.

The Red Light Clothing Exchange
3590 SE Hawthorne Blvd.
(503) 963-8888
http://redlightclothingexchange.com

Red Light is on the Hawthorne strip and is beloved of hipsters, and others, throughout the city. Here you will find an outstanding selection of vintage clothing, as well as contemporary consumer-tested fashions. We always find good leather jackets and evening wear here, but like all resale shops, you'll have to visit for yourself.

Children's Resale

New regulations about lead have made it harder to manage children's resale, but there are nonetheless some excellent shops specializing in gently used children's items. Many of these also carry new (lead-free) items as well. There are numerous children's resale shops in neighborhoods throughout the area. Below are a few of our favorites.

Baby and Me Outlet—Hillsboro
3207 NW Glencoe Rd.
Hillsboro, OR 97123
(503) 846-1402
www.babyandmepdx.com

Beezoo Exchange
2390 NW Thurman St.
(503) 241-2800
www.beezooexchange.com

bella stella
2751 NE Broadway
(503) 284-4636
www.bellastellaresale.com

Daisies & Dinos Resale and Consignment
3432 SE Milwaukie Ave.
(971) 544-7798
www.goodcleankidstuff.com

Hoot-N-Annie
7850 SW Barbur Blvd.
(503) 548-4668
www.hoot-n-annie.com

Sweet Peas
8235 SE 13th Ave.
(503) 233-1153
www.sweetpearesale.com

Savvy Plus
3204 SE Hawthorne Blvd.
(503) 231-7116
www.savvyplus.com

Savvy Plus has cornered a niche market: This shop has outstanding jewelry as well as upscale women's clothing in size 12 and up. The consignment section is excellent, and they also carry new clothing in attractive natural fibers (though as you might imagine, this is not nearly as cheap).

Time Bomb Vintage
3540 SE Division St.
(503) 922-9745
www.etsy.com/shop/timebombvintage

Time Bomb specializes in clothes and accessories—especially shoes—from the '70s and '80s. They have a great selection of menswear as well. The shop is so cute and well organized; the owners live in the neighborhood and could not be nicer; and the selection is hand-curated with a discerning eye. They are not the cheapest vintage store in Portland, but they have good values.

Well Suited
2401 NE Broadway St.
(503) 284-5939
www.wellsuitedpdx.com

Men's clothes, shoes, and accessories are the specialty of this resale and consignment shop on Northeast Broadway. They also offer excellent tailoring. This is the place to come for job interview suits, special occasions, and general male wardrobe refreshment at excellent prices—everything is contemporary and stylish, and the shop is a pleasure to be in.

CONSIGNMENT & **THRIFT** STORES

Better Bargains Thrift Store
10209 NE Sandy Blvd.
(503) 254-1060

Better Bargains is an old-fashioned thrift store that carries everything you would want and many things you would not want. If you do any thrifting, you already know that to have the best experience, you have to do two paradoxical things: Have a list of things you are always looking for (which helps you avoid simply accumulating clutter) and be open to what you happen upon. In this way, you can maximize your Better Bargains experience. They are usually better for household items rather than clothing—I have gotten my best vintage sewing supplies from here—but you never know what you will find. They have weekly markdowns—you can follow these on Facebook.

Goodwill
Multiple locations
http://locator.goodwill.org

The Columbia-Willamette Goodwill has been a national leader in reinventing the thrift store shopping experience, providing clean, well-lit, well-organized thrifting experiences for more than a decade. This is good because it has promoted reusing and recycling, provided jobs, improved retail experience, and delighted the hearts of cheap people all over the Portland Metro area. It has also contributed to higher prices, and as eBay has standardized prices and removed information barriers, Goodwill has been able to take advantage of their donations and target them to different markets. For example, the Hawthorne Goodwill has a greater share of things like sets of Starburst Franciscan china and Pucci-inspired dresses. The Goodwill Store on 10th has designer clothes and high-end home decor objects. But Goodwill seems to be growing under this business model, so good for them. Even with higher prices, you can still find great deals, however, and they have markdown specials consistently. Along with clothing, you will find shoes, bags, books, housewares, furniture, and everything else under the sun.

Goodwill Outlet
1750 SE Ochoco St., Milwaukie
(503) 230-2076

The Goodwill Outlets are for the truly hardcore. It's where the stuff too skeezy for the Goodwill stores is temporarily held before it heads out to landfill and beyond. These too have been changed in recent years by the advent of eBay and the popularity of vintage stores, so you will be competing with the professionals. Still, it can be worth it if you are patient and brave. Be sure to wear gloves, don't wear sandals, and bring the hand sanitizer (or wear a hazmat suit). The anthropological observations alone make a trip worthwhile—your fellow shoppers will be territorial, and don't leave your cart unattended. You pay by the pound for most items, starting at $1.49 per pound for 50 pounds and under. On some items (such as furniture) you can get quotes rather than paying by the pound (this is advised). Do be careful as you sift through the bins—they can be filled with really dirty things. Once one of our friends found a garbage bag full of leaves—and that is not the worst thing we have heard about. But there are enough tales of people reselling vintage textiles on eBay for 5,000 times what they paid for them that everyone keeps coming back for more. A second area location is at 2920 SW 234th Ave., Hillsboro (503-649-5424).

Lounge Lizard

1310 SE Hawthorne Blvd.
(503) 232-7575
www.loungelizard.com

Lounge Lizard carries 20th-century vintage furniture, clothing, and other resale home decor, furnishing, and clothing items. They have an especially impressive lighting collection. If you are looking for strange animal-shaped lamps circa 1958 or the lamp shaped like a woman's leg from *A Christmas Story*, Lounge Lizard is your best bet. One special feature: They have very cheap delivery prices, which is a godsend if you are living the low-car lifestyle.

Rerun

707 NE Fremont St.
(503) 517-3786
www.portlandrerun.com

Rerun offers higher-end resale and consignment—it's especially great for furniture, but you will also find great stuff for children, dishes and other tableware, small electronics and appliances, clothing, jewelry, and, well, everything else. It's essentially a full-service consignment shop. If you don't find it here, you don't really need it. You can sell your stuff too.

Value Village

5050 SE 82nd Ave.
(503) 771-5472
www.valuevillage.com

Value Village is not unlike Goodwill—it's a favorite for Halloween and theater costumes, housewares, resale and vintage clothing, toys, and so on. If you register on their website, you can get member discounts and printable coupons, making the deals that much sweeter. This is one organization that is still connected to a local nonprofit: in this case, The Arc of Multnomah County. Additional area locations are at 18625 SE McLoughlin Blvd., Milwaukie (503-653-7333); and 12060 SW Main, Tigard (503-684-1982).

Village Merchants

3360 SE Division St.
(503) 234-6343

Couponing, Portland Style

It's fun to watch episodes of *Extreme Couponing* to see people come back from the grocery store slightly wealthier than when they left home. Couponing—let us stop and meditate on the use of "coupon" as a verb, which indicates something profound about the way we live now, though I am not sure what—is also a sport we play here in Portland. It is made easier by two resources in particular.

The first is **Frugal Living Northwest** (www.frugallivingnw.com). This combination blog and e-mail list makes couponing much easier—the savvy women who write it guide you through national deals at places like Amazon as well as the fantastic sales on organic green beans at New Seasons. The coupons, deals, and posts are tailored to audiences in Oregon and Southwest Washington. You can go to their site, sign up for e-mails, follow on Twitter, or get the RSS feed. However you get your information, you will be up to date on bargains galore, and you will have plenty of time left over for doing things that are more interesting than clipping coupons—so you save in multiple ways.

The **Chinook Book** (www.chinookbook.net) is another great resource for area residents. It's sold as a fund-raiser at many schools and nonprofits, but you can also pick them up around town—for example, at New Seasons (they take $5 off if you wait until after the holiday season). The Chinook Book is reminiscent of the popular entertainment coupon books that one sees nationally, and here in Portland as well, but it has a "green," local, and sustainable focus. It costs $20, and it has more than 400 coupons and other deals, including mobile coupons for your iPhone and iPad. It more than pays for itself if you use it for discounts on groceries, decor, gardening, and home repair—and it's almost an investment when you use it for discounts on travel, yoga, theater tickets, train fare, and other things that are often rather expensive and that don't usually show up in other coupon books. Where else would you find a coupon for $5 off Birkenstock repair?

This neighborhood gem is worth a trip from wherever you are. Like Rerun, it offers a full range of used and consigned household items and garments. The value of a shop like this is that they don't take everything, so the merchandise has already been curated and you have less work to find what you want. It used to be that the prices reflected this extra work, but Goodwill's prices have increased, so they are now competitive. I have an embarrassing number of items from this shop, and other people have bought an embarrassing number of things that used to be mine. Their kitchen section is very good, and they always have a large selection of furniture.

William Temple House Thrift Store
2230 NW Glisan St.
(503) 222-3328
www.williamtemple.org/store.html

William Temple House is an old-fashioned charity thrift shop and carries furniture and appliances, as well as clothing and decor. You won't find children's items though—they have stopped accepting them. But for other items, you will find pretty cheap prices.

GEAR ON THE CHEAP

Next Adventure
426 SE Grand Ave.
(503) 233-0706
http://nextadventure.net

Next Adventure is a mecca for outdoorsy Portlanders, who flock here for the best deals in the city on equipment for winter sports of every variety, climbing, backpacking, disc golf, hiking, camping, biking, and all the clothing you need for these various pursuits. Their prices are low because they have many closeout and recycled things. They have an outstanding winter sports clearance sale every spring as well, where you can get sweet deals on snowboards, skis, and everything else. They carry excellent brands, from familiar names such as Atomic or Marmot or Teva, to European lines such as LaFuma. The best deals are in the basement: That's where they have the most discounted prices and much used equipment and apparel. They also have a store just for paddle sports one block east of their main store at 704 SE Washington (503-445-9435). You don't even have to be a big outdoors person to find value here: It's fantastic for back-to-school messenger bags, birthday party favors like flashlights or carabiners, and winter woolies. In addition to all this bargain goodness, you can rent equipment there, you can sell your gear there, and you can have your skis and snowboards tuned up there. Plus everyone working there is really nice.

Play It Again Sports
9244 SW Beaverton-Hillsdale Hwy.
(503) 292-4552

Our local member of the national chain, Play It Again Sports is the go-to spot for great deals on a huge variety of sporting equipment, and you can trade or sell your gear there too. It's the perfect place to replace your Ben Hogan P139 putter that your wife accidentally sold at the yard sale.

River City Bicycle Outlet
534 SE Belmont St.
(503) 446-2205

Portland has dozens of bike shops, and many of them carry bikes that cost as much as some cars, making life disappointing for cheap people. We can get cool discounted Chrome waterproof bags at Next Adventure, but not the bikes to carry them on. The good people of River City Bicycles, however, have opened a fantastic outlet to sell closeouts, overstocks, and similar limited edition bikes that they don't carry at their main store. The store is helpfully organized by bike size. Why aren't all bike stores this organized?

DISCOUNT **SHOPS** & OUTLETS

City Liquidators
823 SE 3rd Ave.
(503) 238-1367
www.cityliquidators.com

City Liquidators advertises itself as a home and office furnishings liquidator, which it indeed is, but the store carries many, many other items as well, from ashtrays to Zodiac life rafts, all at rock-bottom prices. The first floor of this cavernous warehouse is stuffed with the smaller items, while the second floor is full of furniture. As in many such places, you must shop with patience—there is a lot of stuff and much of it you may not actually want to bring home. But there are deals to be had.

Columbia Sportswear Outlet
1323 SE Tacoma St., Sellwood
(503) 238-0118

Columbia Sportswear is our homegrown outdoor apparel manufacturer—they make excellent outdoor exercise, leisure, sports, and casual apparel, and you can get it much more cheaply at the outlets. A second location is at 3 Monroe Pkwy., Lake Oswego (503-636-6593).

Hanna Andersson Outlet
7 Monroe Pkwy., Lake Oswego
(503) 697-1953

Hanna Andersson makes exceptionally high-quality Scandinavian-style children's clothing in beautiful cotton and other natural fibers—and they make nice clothes for adults as well. The cozy long johns, tights, and casual wear can be had for reduced prices at the outlet in Lake Oswego.

Nordstrom Rack
Downtown
245 SW Morrison St.
(503) 299-1815

Even die-hard nonconsumers sometimes want to buy something that no one else has ever worn before. In these cases, the Nordstrom Rack can be an excellent choice—this outlet for last season's styles and overstocks provides some great values. The downtown Rack does not carry children's clothing, but you'll find a great selection for kids at Clackamas (8930 SE Sunnyside Rd., 503-654-5415) or Tanasbourne (18100 Northwest Evergreen Pkwy., 503-439-0900). All 3 locations have superb shoe selections, with mouthwatering markdowns. Other markdowns can also be impressive: I once bought an Armani jacket at the downtown Rack for $100. Its original price was $1,100. I love telling that story.

Title Wave
216 NE Knott St.
(503) 988-5021
www.multcolib.org/titlewave

Title Wave sells discards from the Multnomah County Library, and we have gotten some sweet, sweet deals here. Prices for paperbacks start at about $1 and go up from there. Hardbacks begin at about $2. They also have audio books, CDs, DVDs, and multiple other forms of media, including magazines. They even have some ultra bargains for 25 cents.

DO-**IT**-YOURSELF

All frugalisti know that it's usually much cheaper to do home projects yourself, except of course when you are making false economies and you end up making problems worse. Here are some resources for the times when you are thinking clearly about your skills.

Free Geek
1731 SE 10th Ave.
(503) 232-9350
www.freegeek.org

Free Geek is an organization dedicated to providing computers and technology instruction to as many people as possible. They take old computers and peripherals and repurpose them. As part of this endeavor, they have a really cheap retail store, where you can get PC and Macintosh machines and supporting equipment—mice, keyboards, power supplies, scanners, printers . . . you get the idea. They use open source programs and offer lots of tech support. If you volunteer, you can get things even more cheaply. Where else can you get an $80 iMac? Okay, it won't perform exactly like the latest G5, but still. They also will take, wipe, and dismantle, reuse, or recycle your stupid old computer stuff that you don't know what to do with.

Hippo Hardware and Trading Company
1040 E. Burnside St.
(503) 231-1444
www.hippohardware.com

Hippo Hardware was ahead of the curve in terms of spotting the repressed desire for rehabbing old houses in Portland, and they got into the game early. They have great prices on plumbing fixtures, doors, lighting fixtures, and salvaged items. They will trade for credit or cash, so if you are replacing the doorknobs in your Craftsman, you might take them here.

Metro Paint Store
4825 N. Basin Ave.
(503) 234-3000
www.oregonmetro.gov

The Metro Paint Store sells recycled latex paint for cheap—from $32 to $47 for a 5-gallon bucket, depending on the color (you can also get deeply discounted composters here). The drawback is that the color palette is somewhat limited, though it is expanding, and because it is recycled, it might not be as consistent in its quality as other commercially available paints. But if you need cheap paint, and you want to do your part for the planet, this could be a good option.

Old Portland Hardware
4035 SE Division St.
(503) 234-7380
www.oldportlandhardware.com

This fabulous architectural salvage shop carries the things you need to make your old house functional and pretty. They also have dollar bins, and they are amenable to trading and bartering. Sometimes they will hang a "Free" sign by a small area off their parking lot, which will have odds and ends just waiting for someone to take them home for some TLC.

The Rebuilding Center
3625 N. Mississippi Ave.
(503) 331-1877
http://rebuildingcenter.org

This revolutionary business deconstructs houses and other buildings and then sells the salvage here. Since they are ecumenical in what they take apart, you can find salvage from every architectural style and era. Look for doors and windows, as well as fixtures such as sinks. It's also a good resource for yard renovation—they will often carry old bricks or stone. However, luck and patience may be involved—if you are looking for something specific, you may have to return often until is shows up.

Rejuvenation
1100 SE Grand Ave.
(503) 238-1900
www.rejuvenation.com

Rejuvenation is well known nationally for its beautifully designed period lighting fixtures and other house parts, but it is far from cheap—except if you look through their seconds room. There you will find gorgeous things that someone custom-ordered and then decided they didn't like: You can have these things comparatively cheaply. They also have a good salvage section—not as cheap as some places but worth looking over, especially if you live in an old house with tricky fixtures.

SCRAP
2915 NE Martin Luther King Jr. Blvd.
(503) 294-0769
http://scrapaction.org

SCRAP began as a way to provide art supplies to teachers cheaply, but its well-timed start, at the beginning of the crafting revival, has allowed it to expand its scope, mission, and square footage considerably. This shop really does sell scraps of everything: fabric, papers of every weight and variety, things made of plastic, bottle caps, old CDs, old CD jewel cases, notions, leather, thread, yarn, and on and on. It is a thrift store devoted just to stuff for crafting and art projects. You can also have kids' birthday parties here, and they have workshops, volunteer opportunities, and other events for the truly committed.

HEALTH & MEDICAL:
AN APPLE A DAY

"Be careful about reading health books.
You might die of a misprint."

—MARK TWAIN

Whether or not you have insurance, there is nothing cheap about health care. As the national conversation about the state of health care unfolds, it's clear that we have some work to do to figure this out. If you don't have health insurance, the state of Oregon offers a special high-risk plan for those with pre-existing conditions who can't get insurance or those who have exhausted COBRA benefits. You can find out more information on their website: www .omip.state.or.us. In the meantime, you can try not to get sick, but even the healthiest among us can break a bone or pick up some hideous virus from their children. Here are some resources to keep you up and running.

HEALTH CLINICS

Multnomah County Health
http://web.multco.us/health/health-services
(503) 988-5558 (initial primary care appointment)
(503) 988-6942 (dental care for emergencies and for the uninsured)

The Multnomah County Health Department is the front line for public health in the city, doing the hard, fastidious, and mostly unrecognized work of keeping us all safe from horrible infectious diseases. They also, of course, offer health care for low-income people and can help them enroll in the Oregon Health Plan (Oregon's version of Medicaid) and provide many resources for families. Services include health care for adults and children; women's health, including birth control, pregnancy testing, and prenatal care; help with drug and alcohol addiction; mental health; and services for refugees. Importantly, they also provide dental clinics—this is critical, since good dental health has been shown to prevent long-term chronic health problems such cardiovascular disease. The numbers listed above are the ones you should call to make the first appointment. These lines are staffed from 8 a.m. to 5 p.m., Mon through Fri.

ZoomCare Neighborhood Clinics
Multiple locations
www.zoomcare.com

ZoomCare clinics offer a new model of health care: You pay for services directly. (Actually, this is an old model of health care.) This "on-demand" service delivery model offers same-day appointments for urgent and primary care—if, for example, you jammed your finger during basketball practice or if you think you might have strep throat. ZoomCare is excellent not only for people who don't have health insurance, but also for people with catastrophic-coverage insurance—but if you have regular insurance, you can use it too. This is also a great option for people who are visiting Portland and who might otherwise be saddled with enormous bills for seeing an out-of-network provider. All visits start with a basic fee; lab tests, X-rays, vaccinations, and other services are added on to the bill, à la carte style. Unlike most health-care organizations, if you are paying for ZoomCare yourself, you pay less: $99 per visit, plus extras. If your insurance company is paying, the base visits cost $129. All fees are listed on their website, so you can get an idea about what you might be paying for.

You conveniently can schedule by phone or online for same-day services (you can schedule in advance as well). Clinic hours vary from site to site, but generally they are open from about 9 a.m. (sometimes earlier or later) to about 6 p.m., sometimes 7. All clinics are open from 9 a.m. to 6 p.m. on the weekends. More are scheduled to be opened in the near future.

ALTERNATIVE **HEALTH** CARE

National College of Naturopathic Medicine
3025 SW Corbett Ave.
(503) 552-1551
(503) 552-1515 (community clinic information)

Portland has a strong alternative health care community—including a nationally recognized naturopathic medical school, the National College of Naturopathic Medicine. This rigorous program trains naturopaths to the highest standards, as well as conducting peer-reviewed research funded by the National Institutes of Health—and they offer alternative-care clinics for excellent prices. The services include both naturopathic and classical

Chinese medicine, and many insurance plans cover these services. They also provide community clinics that serve low-income people. In addition, the college has a well-priced alternative pharmacy for supplements, herbal medicines, and other items.

SEXUAL **HEALTH**

Multnomah County Health Department STD Clinic
426 SW Stark St., 6th floor
(503) 988-3700
(503) 988-5727 (test results)
http://web.multco.us/health/std-services

Helping citizens to keep it clean, the county health department offers STD testing and treatment regardless of ability to pay or social circumstance or primary language (interpreters are available, including for the hearing-impaired). Services are confidential, and they won't moralize. In addition to testing, they provide free condoms, treatment for many conditions, and various vaccinations. Teenagers are welcome and don't need parental permission. HIV testing is available, with or without accompanying STD testing, and it can be anonymous if you need it to be; they will also connect you with services. The clinic also can test for hepatitis C. You can make an appointment or walk in. Hours are daily from 9 a.m. to 4:15 p.m., except on Wednesday, when they open at 11 a.m. At your visit, you can arrange to get any test results by phone; phone results are available from 1:30 to 4 p.m. Fees are based on a sliding scale—pay something if you can.

Pivot
209 SW 4th Ave.
(503) 445-7699
www.pivotpdx.org

Pivot is a wellness and social center primarily targeting gay, bisexual, and transgender men. They provide free STD and HIV testing. The HIV clinics are on Tuesday evenings, Wednesday midday, and Saturday evenings. During the Tuesday and Wednesday clinics, you can also get tested for other STDs

(Saturday is HIV only). These tests are walk-in, confidential, and anonymous, meaning they won't report your HIV status to anyone official. These screenings are very popular and fill up quickly, so be prepared. Results for STD testing take about a week, but HIV tests produce their results in about 20 minutes. Special, festive youth screenings are offered on the second and fourth Monday of each month from 3 to 7 p.m.—for both men and women under 25. Free condoms are also available.

Planned Parenthood
NE Portland Center
3727 NE Martin Luther King Jr. Blvd.
(888) 875-7820

Planned Parenthood is the provider of choice for many women, offering breast and cervical exams as well as contraception, HIV testing, and testing for STDs. Planned Parenthood also offers LGBT-competent care and services, including testing and other health services for men. Free condoms too. There are 2 locations in Portland, both on the east side of the river. The Southeast Portland location (3231 SE 50th) offers extended women's health services, including treatments for abnormal Pap smears and urinary tract infections. You should pay at the time of service, but they will work with you, even if you are uninsured.

OUTDOOR RECREATION, SPORTS & FITNESS:
CHEAP THRILLS

"If you come to a fork in the road, take it."

—YOGI BERRA

The outdoor lifestyle and natural beauty of Oregon are two of the reasons people migrate to the Northwest, and to Portland in particular. Ninety minutes' drive in any direction can put you in the heart of the wilderness. And . . . this beauty is cheap! It's not expensive to immerse yourself in all this natural wonder—at least, if you aren't caught up in showing off the latest props. Outdoor sports have a well-earned reputation for being very expensive, and there are plenty of ways to spend lots of money on gear. In the Shopping chapter, you'll find where to locate great bargains on equipment. In this chapter, you'll read about where to use it.

CHEAP & **FREE** RESOURCES

Before you heed the siren call of Oregon's wilderness, you should check out the amazingly useful resources offered by the **Nature of the Northwest Information Center** (www.naturenw.org), an office co-sponsored by the U.S. Forest Service and the Oregon Department of Geology. This center provides maps, guidance, and great links to critical information for frugal outdoor enthusiasts. Some of these are even free! More information about using these resources is found in the Escaping the City chapter.

GOLF

Half the reason we stayed in Oregon after graduate school was so my husband could play golf as cheaply as and as often as possible. Here are his secrets to making it to the 19th hole without falling into the hole.

Portland has excellent municipal golf courses, and they are some of the most challenging and attractive in the state. It's easy to see why the area has an outstanding reputation for golf: The courses are beautiful, offering gorgeous views, communion with nature (fortuitously, sometimes you see eagles!), well-designed courses, and fast greens—at least in summer. Yet this golf goodness can be yours for less. Most fees fall in the $25 to $45 range, and discounts are available for weekday and off-season play, as well

Portland Parks & Recreation: Cheap Fitness and Fun

We love our Parks & Recreation programs in Portland, and it's easy to see why. These public resources comprise not just dozens of parks but also attractive recreation and fitness centers and pools, civilized tennis courts, competitive league sports, and lessons to improve any of these activities. The Parks & Recreation department maintains an exceptionally useful web resource (www.portlandonline.com/parks or www.portlandparks.org) that allows you to locate a facility near you, sign up for classes, reserve rooms if necessary, and otherwise organize your fitness time. They also run an excellent Outdoor Recreation Program that includes adventures such as sea kayaking or sailing trips to the San Juan Islands.

Portland Parks & Recreation also has league sports and drop-in play for a variety of sports, including soccer, cross-country, swimming, tennis, baseball, track and field, basketball and more. These lower-priced alternatives allow people of all ages and skill levels to compete or just play informally.

A complete listing of the recreation centers is found in Appendix B. They are some of the best deals for fitness in town—$5 per visit for adults, and cheaper if you buy in bulk. They include weight rooms, aerobic equipment, pools, gyms, and depending on the facility, rock climbing walls and other cool amenities. Unlike the gym membership that you never use but still pay for, here you only pay when you visit.

as afternoon and twilight rates. Other savings come from the fact that carts are rarely required, so not only do you save on cart rental but you can actually get some exercise. Also, many area courses offer discounted greens fees for juniors, seniors, or both. Senior players can get a discount card for the municipal courses. Check **www.portlandpublicgolf.com** for more information.

You can make tee times 6 days to 1 hour in advance for the municipal courses—Eastmoreland, Heron Lakes, Red Tail, and Rose City—by reserving them on a central website, www.portlandpublicgolf.com, or by calling the pro shops directly, listed below.

Note: Nonmetal spikes are the only kind allowed on most Portland golf courses.

Broadmoor

3509 NE Columbia Blvd.
(503) 281-1337
www.broadmoor-1931.com

This is not a municipal course but it is nevertheless one of the best golf values in Portland. This 18-hole, par-72 course expands over 220 acres, with plenty of water hazards and trees to dodge. The course is sited along the Broadmoor Lake and Slough, which gives you something pretty to look at while you're waiting for your partner to find his ball.

Eastmoreland

2425 SE Bybee Blvd.
(503) 775-2900
www.portlandpublicgolf.com (tee times)
www.eastmorelandgolfcourse.com

Eastmoreland is the oldest golf course in the city and a true favorite, with lovely mature trees and lush flowering shrubs. It is flanked by Crystal Springs Lake, Crystal Springs Rhododendron Gardens, and Johnson Creek, adding to the beauty of the course. The course is also the site of the annual city championship.

Glendoveer Golf Course

14015 NE Glisan St.
(503) 253-7507
www.golfglendoveer.com

This par-73 course has 36 regulation holes across 280 acres of varied terrain. The east course is 6,296 yards, while the west course is 5,922 yards, and along both you will find plenty of hills, trees, water, wind, and rough.

Heron Lakes Golf Course

3500 N. Victory Blvd.
(503) 289-1818
www.portlandpublicgolf.com (tee times)
www.heronlakesgolf.com

Heron Lakes comprises 2 links-style courses near the confluence of the Willamette and Columbia Rivers. These beautiful courses are the Greenback (6,621 yards) and the Great Blue (6,916 yards); this latter is the crown jewel in Portland Parks' municipal golf program. (Both were designed by noted golf architect Robert Trent Jones II.) Playing these courses you will encounter bunkers, uneven lies, and lots of water, as well as bald eagles, Canada geese, and great blue herons. Book your tee time 6 days in advance; they fill up quickly.

Lake Oswego Golf Course
17525 SW Stafford Rd., Lake Oswego
(503) 636-8228
www.lakeoswegogolf.org

This executive municipal course is challenging for its short game. With just 2,693 yards, there are no golf carts here, but lessons are available.

Red Tail Golf Course
8200 SW Scholls Ferry Rd.
(503) 646-5166
www.portlandpublicgolf.com (tee times)
www.golfredtail.com

Red Tail is noted for a couple of important things: its excellent drainage (an important feature in Oregon) and its excellent education and training of the current and future generations of golfers. This 7,100-yard championship 18-hole public golf course maintains its fast greens all through the winter, so it is popular all year long. Book in advance.

Rose City Golf Course
2200 NE 71st Ave.
(503) 253-4744
www.portlandpublicgolf.com (tee times)
www.rosecitygc.com

Rose City is another older course, one that is not only good-looking but also challenging in all the right ways. You'll encounter long par-4s, and the trees surrounding the fairways will keep you alert. This 6,520-yard course has a reputation for having 2 of the hardest finishing holes in town.

SKI **AREAS**

Winter sports are notoriously expensive. Growing up, my friends scoffed at the people with the latest gear; at that time, it was a well-established fact that the best skiers schussed down the mountain wearing old sweaters and jeans. Luckily, waterproof fabrics have improved and gotten cheaper, and now even The Frugal can avail themselves of them.

Mt. Hood, the state's highest peak at 11,239 feet, has multiple ski resorts and cross-country trails, most of which are less than 2 hours from your front door.

One thing that every winter sport enthusiast needs is a **Sno-Park permit** prominently displayed in the windshield. You need this whether you are heading up to the resorts for downhill or snowboarding or whether you are pulling off into the designated areas for parking for cross-country and snowshoe trails. It is very expensive to keep the roads clear so we can take advantage of these beautiful mountains, and so the State of Oregon asks us all to pitch in to cover the costs—although, of course, being the state, it's not really optional. You'll get a ticket if you don't have the permit. They cost $25 per year, $9 for 3 days, or $4 for 1 day, and you can purchase one at ski areas, outdoor stores, or DMV offices, as well as at most local businesses on the way up to Mt. Hood on US 26. Merchants are allowed to tack on service fees, so the cheapest option is the DMV—and the DMV is cash or check only. Note that "Sno-Park" means "Parking in the Snow," and not, as one exasperated mom who stopped to ask for directions with a minivan full of wretched toddlers thought, a park in the snow.

Mt. Hood Meadows
FR 3555, 6 miles north of the junction of Hwy. 35 and US 26
(503) 337-2222, (800) SKI-HOOD
www.skihood.com

Known as "Meadows," this ski area is popular because it's close enough to town but it's on the east side of the mountain, meaning that it's sunnier and more protected from the chilly east wind that shudders through Portland during the winter. There are 10 chair lifts, including 3 high-speed quads, and 82 trails. It's best for beginners and experts: There are several easy runs as well as one double black diamond.

How to Save Money on Winter Sports Gear

Savvy skiers and snowboarders are well acquainted with the ways to acquire inexpensive equipment. One gem is the **Mt. Hood Snosport Swap** (http://mhsss.com), an annual event held in early October where you can get consumer-tested and otherwise discounted gear. You can sell your old board as long as it's in good shape. Local winter sports dealers also participate, so you can get beautiful deals on last year's models. There's a small admission fee (families can get in for $6; kids under 12 are free; and everyone else costs $3), and if you sell your stuff, you pay a fee of $1 per item plus 20 percent of the sales price. Or you can take the tax deduction and just donate your stuff. Bring plastic or cash; no checks (an ATM is available). All proceeds go to support the West Linn High School snowboarding team and the fearless Mt. Hood Ski Patrol.

REI is also a favorite—sometimes their sales are incredible—as is Next Adventure (see the Shopping chapter). You can also rent gear cheaply at Next Adventure and at Portland State University. Portland State's rentals, which include backpacking and climbing gear, are ridiculously cheap for students, but not too bad for the general public either. You can check out their offerings and price list on their web page: www.pdx.edu/recreation/equipment-rental-center.

Mt. Hood Skibowl

87000 E. US 26 at Government Camp
(503) 272-3206
(503) 222-2695 (info line)
www.skibowl.com

Skibowl is the closest ski area to Portland and thus very, very popular, especially with beginners. Its conditions can be quite different from those further up the mountain. It offers 65 day runs and 34 night runs; the longest run, Skyline Trail, is 3 miles. The top elevation is 5,056, with a vertical drop of about 1,500 feet. The main slope divides in two, and on the alternative trail, you will encounter many jumps, rails, and a half-pipe. Skibowl is particularly noted for its night skiing—it's open every night during the season and two thirds of the runs are lit.

Cheap Lift Tickets

If you want to ski or snowboard but you're short on cash, you still have a number of options. Obviously, the season pass is the best deal if you plan to head up to the mountain a lot; this option will pay for itself the more times you go up. But with season passes at around $400 even at discounted prices, you may want to explore other options. REI (www.rei.com) has partnerships with many of the local ski areas, and these can offer good discounts. Late-season ski-ing—spring skiing, we call it around here—can offer great value, with passes sometimes running at under $100 after Mar 1. Of course, these depend on whether there is any snow. (That said, some ski areas near Portland have skiing nearly year-round!) Perhaps the best value is night skiing at Skibowl (see above). Skibowl is the closest resort to Portland, and you can head up after work and be there in about an hour most of the winter. On the last day of the season—which, to be sure, varies from year to year—several of the resorts offer free skiing all day.

Summit Ski and Snow Play Area
US 26 at the east end of Government Camp
(503) 272-0256
www.summitskiarea.com

Summit Ski and Snow Play Area is the second-oldest resort in the United States. Its gentle vertical slopes are great for beginners, and you see many families here—not just skiing or snowboarding but also for the great tubing hills.

Timberline Lodge and Ski Area
6 miles north of Government Camp, off Forest Road 50
(503) 622-7979
(503) 222-2211 (ski report)
www.timberlinelodge.com

This beautiful resort was built as part of the WPA during the Great Depression, and it has achieved iconic status in the Northwest. Elevation reaches about 8,500 feet, with stunning views on sunny winter days. It's known as a beginning-to-intermediate resort. Timberline claims to have the longest ski season in North America (and who are we to argue?), which means you can utilize those late-season passes.

CROSS-COUNTRY **SKIING** & **SNOWSHOEING**

These low-tech sports are the frugalista's winter sports delight. They require little gear, they don't require expensive lift tickets, they get you out into some of the most beautiful country known to mankind, and you can bring your lunch and a thermos of coffee. What is not to love?

The Mt. Hood wilderness area has miles and miles of groomed trails and US Forest Service roads that are used by snowshoers and skiers. You can see these at the Mt. Hood National Forest website: www.fs.fed.us/r6/mthood. Here you'll find dozens of trails, but they are a little buried in this information-packed site: Once you're at the portal, use the navigation bar on the left to find Recreation, then Winter Sports, then XC Skiing and Snowshoeing. Click on the trail of choice, and you'll find current conditions, as well as tons of information about the trail, including a Google Earth map.

Sno-Park Ski Areas
(503) 986-4000
www.tripcheck.com/pages/spentry.asp

There are 26 Sno-Parks in the Mt. Hood National Forest operated by the Oregon Department of Transportation, and most of them offer access to cross-country skiing and snowshoeing. A couple of the downhill resorts also offer nice groomed trails—for example, Mt. Hood Meadows offers a full-service Nordic center and 15 kilometers of trails for cross-country skiers, but there are fees of up to $10—which is still way cheaper than a lift ticket. The trails below either are at no cost to you or request donations (usually $5).

Teacup Lake
Near Mt. Hood Meadows
www.teacupnordic.org

Pretty Teacup Lake has 12 kilometers of trails groomed for both skating and cross-country skiing. It's 1 mile north of Mt. Hood Meadows, on Highway 35. No dogs or snowshoers allowed, and a $5 donation is requested.

Trillium Lake Snowtrails
Near Government Camp

Trillium Lake offers 6 gorgeous miles of groomed trails around the lake for snowshoers and cross-country skiers. Donations are requested, and Fido can come with you if he's on a leash.

SWIMMING

Tualatin Hills Aquatic Center
Howard M. Terpenning Recreation Complex
15707 SW Walker Rd., Beaverton
(503) 645-7454
www.thprd.org/aquatics/hmtaquatic/home.cfm

This aquatics center is located in the Terpenning Recreation Complex, a sprawling 90-acre park in the Tualatin Hills southwest of Portland. It features a gorgeous 50-meter pool, and it's a favorite for swimming lessons, diving instruction, and other aquatic and fitness fun. Call for drop-in hours. You'll need an ID card from the center to use it. Children who live within the boundaries of the Tualatin Hills Parks and Recreation District pay $2.50 with these ID cards; nonresident children pay $7.50. Adult residents pay $3.50, while nonresident adults pay $10.50. Classes are extra. Residents and nonresidents alike, however, can purchase a discounted "Frequent User" pass for fitness classes.

Portland City Pools
Portland Parks & Recreation has 12 pools, 6 indoor and 6 outdoor, scattered throughout the city, all of which are listed in Appendix B. The outdoor pools are available from Memorial Day through Labor Day and are busy all summer long with free swim, lap swim, swimming lessons, parties, and other events.

For both indoor and outdoor pools, the hours are generally from 6 a.m. to 9 p.m. daily, opening a little later on the weekends. Sometimes pools are reserved for parties, classes, or swim team practice, but they usually manage to keep a few lanes open for adult lap swim. Best of all, swimming is pretty cheap—about $5 for adults, about $3 for those 3 to 17, and free for kids 2 and younger. The information line for aquatics is (503) 823-7946, or you can visit www.portlandparks.org.

TENNIS

The Portland Parks & Recreation Department has close to 100 tennis courts. Some of these are in disrepair (though as long as you don't trip and hurt yourself, they can be good for practicing, since they are not popular). Some are gorgeous and have been recently upgraded. Some have practice walls. All of the outdoor courts in public parks, regardless of their condition, are free. Sometimes they are reserved for local tournament play or high school tennis team practice.

Irving Park
NE 7th Avenue and Fremont Street

These sumptuous courts are well-lit—and very popular, so be prepared to wait.

Laurelhurst Park
SE 39th Avenue and Stark Street

These busy courts are for day use only—there's no lighting. But they are pretty.

Mt. Tabor Park
Mt. Tabor has two sets of courts, on the west side of the park, with a nice view of the reservoir, and on the east side of park, with a view of Mt. Hood. You pick. The west side courts are popular and have lights for evening play.

YOGA

Yoga is a very Portland activity, and a very Portland occupation is being a yoga teacher. This translates into cheap yoga for you, because there are a lot of teachers in training who need to practice on you—and these classes are often paid for by donation, which is good because yoga is not cheap! You will need to be patient (repeat the mantra: Every person is my teacher), but you can still get a great yoga experience and help out the budding yogis. The following studios have community classes that are either discounted or donation. Be sure to check the schedule, because times and prices may change.

The Bhaktishop
2500 SE 26th Ave.
(503) 244-0108
http://thebhaktishop.com

Bhaktishop specializes in "juicy flow" vinyasa, but they also have meditation, hatha yoga, and a wonderful free Kirtan singing class. Donation classes are on Tues at 7 p.m. and Thurs at 4 p.m.

Yoga Shala
1812 NE Alberta St.
(503) 281-4452
www.yogashalapdx.com

Yoga Shala offers a variety of practices, from basic hatha and vinyasa to alternative styles such as "Shadow" yoga, which focuses on perfecting stance and breath (insofar as we can perfect anything). They hold many, many lectures and teacher training is a major component of their 2 studios. They have open practices for $5 and drop-in discounts for some classes of $8. Their second location is at 3249 SE Division St. (503-963-9642).

Yoga Union
2043 SE 50th Ave.
(503) 235-9642
www.yogaunioncwc.com

Yoga Union features a very popular hot yoga series, but they also have free drop-in vinyasa classes on Thurs at 4 p.m. We also like their excellent restorative yoga classes.

NOSEBLEED **SEATS:** SPECTATOR **SPORTS**

Portland Timbers
Jeld-Wen Field
1844 SW Morrison St.
(503) 553-5400 (information)
(503) 553-5555 (tickets)
www.portlandtimbers.com

The Portland Timbers are our new Major League Soccer expansion team in beautifully remodeled Jeld-Wen Field. John Spencer is the head coach, Gavin Wilkinson the general manager. In the team's first year, season tickets sold out in about 30 seconds. Single seats can run as much as $125, but the "Value Terrace" has small blocks of single seats for $8, $9, and $12. Otherwise, general admission tickets run about $20 to $25—if you can get them. We expect that as the team settles in, there will be discounts and promotions. Stay tuned.

The Portland Trailblazers
The Rose Garden, 1 Center Ct.
(503) 234-9291
(503) 321-3211 (events hotline)
www.nba.com/blazers

The Portland Trailblazers are the major sports event in town, kind of like our collective high school team. You can spend thousands on box seats, but the cheap seats will set you back about $10. Ordinary tickets are usually available even on game day, depending on the opponent. You can often find refreshments-plus-tickets deals and other promotions too. Tickets are available from the Rose Garden box office and from Ticketmaster, (503) 224-4400, which is also partially owned by Paul Allen. The truly cheap will take public transportation and avoid pricey parking charges: The MAX drops you off right in front of the Rose Garden.

Portland Winter Hawks
Western Hockey League
Portland Memorial Coliseum & Rose Garden, 1 Center Ct.
(503) 238-6366
www.winterhawks.com

The Winter Hawks, known locally as the Hawks, have been playing in Portland since 1976. They are a JV team for the NHL. Hawks tickets start at about $15, but there are many discounts available, and $15 is pretty cheap if you like hockey.

Safeway Classic Golf Tournament
(503) 626-2711
(503) 287-LPGA (ticket sales)
http://safewayclassic.com

The Safeway Classic is held at the Pumpkin Ridge golf course. It is one of the oldest events on the LPGA (Ladies' Professional Golf Association) tour. This exciting tournament has been in Portland since it started in 1972, and its large purse brings out the LPGA stars and interested fans alike. You can see it for cheap if you watch the specials from Safeway prior to the event—while tickets are usually $10 to $25, there are many promotions that will lower the price, especially for kids.

BEAUTY SERVICES:
CHEAP IS IN THE EYE
OF THE BEHOLDER

*"The problem with beauty is that it's like
being born rich and getting poorer."*

—JOAN COLLINS

Upkeep is expensive. Plucking brows, touching up roots, keeping the split ends at bay, keeping your skin clear and polished and your nails unchipped: It adds up very fast. Throw in the massage you require to abate the stress of spending so much money on personal services and you can really blow your budget. Fortunately, there are trainees and other dedicated souls all over the city willing to keep you looking fresh at bargain prices. And you are also helping out these civic-minded people—dedicated to beautifying the citizens of Portland and beyond—by giving them more experience.

BEAUTY **SCHOOL** DROP-IN

Looking good can be expensive—stylists and estheticians are highly trained entrepreneurs who know how to capitalize on our desire to look great and feel better. Yet once they were mere fledgling stylists. You can use this to your advantage by having your treatments done at one of the great cosmetology schools in the area, while these clever entrepreneurs are still in training. One note of caution: You should be aware that you are in a school, so services that would take less time in a salon staffed by professionals will take longer, especially if you are a volunteer hair model, trading your time for their learning experience. Do not be in a hurry and make sure you've fed the parking meter appropriately. And you may not have much say in the kind of cut or style you want if you are a volunteer model. If this scares you, skip the modeling and stick with booking an appointment at the salon. Still, life is short—maybe it's time for pink hair.

Aveda Institute Portland
325 NW 13th Ave.
(503) 294-6000
www.avedapdx.com/guest_services.php

The Catch: Students are encouraged to hawk Aveda products as part of their training, so be polite about the up-sell at the end.

The Aveda line is renowned for its aromatic properties and its commitment to organic and sustainable ingredients and materials wherever possible. Their Portland training institute is also known for its rigorous curriculum—

students must really know their chemistry, for example, and the instructors are deeply experienced stylists, estheticians, and massage professionals who tolerate no slacking from their students. The result is that you can feel confident that your hair color and other treatments will look pretty amazing. Haircuts here start about $10, color at $35, nail services at $5 (French polish only; $12 for manicures), makeup services at $8, and spa services at $25. The latter include both facials and body treatments. Aveda Institute students are always looking for hair and makeover models to practice on, and you can find opportunities on Craigslist or by signing up with them on their website. In this case, your haircut will be entirely free.

Beau Monde
1221 SW 12th Ave.
(503) 226-7355
www.beaumondecollege.com/pages/public-salon

Beau Monde has an excellent reputation—the avant-garde of the cosmetology world in Portland, with internships in Japan and Europe available to their students and alumni. They are independent of any particular product line, belonging instead to the well-respected and longstanding Pivot Point consortium of cosmetology schools. What this means for you is that your student stylist is being held to extremely high standards. Prices are still just as reasonable here, however. Haircuts start at $6 if you skip the shampoo and conditioner (which they can do because they don't need to sell you any product), while full color and highlights can be had for $51. Beau Monde emphasizes hair artistry, so this is the go-to place if you want bright blue hair, which you can get for about $40. They also offer a full range of cosmetic services, including lash tints, waxing, and makeup.

On Wednesday, for an extra dollar you can partake of a menu of extra services—for example, if you're there for a haircut, for $1 more, you can get a facial. Seniors can get 10 percent discounts every day, and if you're going to the prom or any other high school dance, you can have a mani-pedi, updo, and your makeup done for $30. Just pray that your dance is not on a Friday or you might not have enough time after school to take advantage of this fabulous offer. They helpfully state up front on the website the expected duration of the appointment; this is useful because it's a good reminder that, in spite of the obvious professionalism, you are still in a school.

Bella Institute

2215 SE Division St.
(503) 236-5600
www.bellainstitute.com/portland-beauty-salon

This newly remodeled cosmetology school in Southeast Portland offers $4 haircuts and 3-color weaves for $35. That's about $100 less than the standard 3-color weave. Blowouts are just $2.50. They also offer waxing, nail services, and makeup for equally reasonable prices. Packages are available—for example, if you're going to the prom, you can get nails, makeup, and your updo done for $22. Even better, on Wednesday, anyone 55 and older receives a 25 percent discount. These are sweet, sweet deals, people.

Paul Mitchell—The School

234 SW Broadway
(503) 222-7687
www.paulmitchelltheschoolportland.com/html/guestservices/index.cfm

Paul Mitchell offers extensive training in hair and style services based on their well-respected product line. Their salon services are thus based on these products and require some interpretation if you are making an appointment—what is a Shoe Shine, in the context of hair? It starts at $19.95, in any case. Even if you want a simple haircut, do you want an adaptive haircut for $12.95 or a creative haircut for $15.95? Be sure to ask, so you know what you're actually getting. Regardless of the nomenclature, the services are very well priced: a Sea Salt Glow body treatment can be had for $35; waxing prices top out at $35; a simple polish change is but $5, while the spa mani-pedi is $27.95. They also offer extensive facial services, including excellent prices on microdermabrasion packages.

Portland Beauty School

8230 NE Siskiyou St.
(503) 255-6303
www.portlandbeautyschool.com/service-menu.html

Portland Beauty School offers a full range of hair, skin, and nail treatments using a variety of lines (Paul Mitchell, Dermatologica), and they also offer advanced training to their students. This means that you can get hair extensions for, well, cheaper than other places. (You'll need to work it out with them—the price depends on what they have to work with.) Otherwise, hair styling prices start at $2 for a bang trim and $5 haircuts, with color and chemical treatments beginning at about $20; brow waxes for $6; facials starting at $9; and basic pedicures for $12. Fill out their online survey and you may be eligible for a free service.

CHEAP **BARBERS** & SALONS

Bishops Barbershops
Multiple locations
www.bishopsbs.com

Bishops is a popular, no-frills local chain that offers hair and barbering services at affordable prices. The vibe is fun and upbeat; you walk in and put your name on the list and wait a few minutes. They aren't as cheap as the schools, but then again, their stylists are already trained. The value comes in the à la carte pricing—if you just want a haircut, you don't need to pay for the shampoo and conditioning treatment. Hot shave service starts at $19. Haircuts start at $12 for clippers-only and $25 if your tresses are long and luxurious. One the one hand, you will pay $3 for the shampoo and $5 for the blow-dry, so after awhile things could add up. On the other hand, you will get a cold Miller High Life for free if you are 21 or older. Check out their website for information on their many area locations.

Kuts 4 Kids
4423 SE Hawthorne Blvd.
(503) 238-1568

Kuts 4 Kids (& Adults) specializes in haircuts for children—many a small girl has gone in with long unruly hair and come out with tidy beribboned French braids; many a small boy has gone in with curly baby locks and come out looking considerably older. They know how to soothe scared children and comfort teary-eyed parents who can't believe it's all going by so fast and are sad to see the baby curls go, all for around $14. There are toys and a little television playing cartoons to keep the siblings occupied. You will need to make an appointment—they fill up fast, and this is an owner-occupied place, not a chain salon, so the stylists (who could not be sweeter) have a loyal clientele. Even though they specialize in children's haircuts, they will gladly cut adult hair too, so you can get the whole family in there if you need to.

Rudy's Barbershop
212 NW 13th Ave.
(503) 525-2900
http://rudysbarbershop.com

Rudy's is a west-coast chain originally founded in Seattle. Not unlike Bishops, they specialize in quick haircuts with à la carte pricing; you can call ahead, but catering to customers is not really their thing. If you walk in, put your name on the list, and be patient while you wait a bit, you'll have a fine experience for not too much cash. So just walk in. Your hair will look great. A second location is at 3015 SE Division (503-232-3850).

CHEAP **RELAXATION**

Portland not only has many hair-cutting schools, but we also have many schools that offer training in massage, acupuncture, and other services. For this reason, there are many people competing to get their training hours in so they can become licensed. This benefits you because you can get spa services for cheap!

East-West College of the Healing Arts
525 NE Oregon St.
(503) 233-6500
www.eastwestcollege.com

East-West College probably has the largest and most established training program in massage in the area. This accredited program teaches a range of bodywork and massage techniques, with an underlying foundation of Swedish massage, which advanced trainees then happily practice on you in their student clinic. The clinic charges $25 for a 45-minute massage. Appointment times vary—however, they are usually offered daily at 11:40 a.m. and 1, 3:10, 4:30, 6:40, and 8 p.m. The instructors also have a professional clinic—they charge $50 for a 60-minute massage and $70 for 90 minutes, and this is also a really good deal comparatively speaking. You can schedule an appointment at the number above; just be sure to ask for either the student clinic or the professional clinic.

Oregon School of Massage
9500 SW Barbur Blvd., Ste. 100
(503) 892-5753
http://oregonschoolofmassage.com/

This longtime, accredited massage therapy program is responsible for many of the excellent therapists working throughout the area. Establish a relationship early by using their massage clinic. The hours are somewhat subscribed, but the prices cannot be beat: 1 hour of Swedish massage is $30 (Wed afternoon at 1:45 and at 3:30; Sat morning at 8:45 and 10:30); 1 hour and 15 minutes of Shiatsu also costs $30 (Tues at 1:45 and 3:30 p.m.); and a beautiful 2 hours and 40 minutes of Shiatsu massage costs a mere $50 (Tues at 2 p.m.). Your muscles will thank you.

Portland Beauty School
8230 NE Siskiyou St.
(503) 255-6303
www.portlandbeautyschool.com/service-menu.html

In addition to the beauty services listed above, Portland Beauty School also offers massage services, since they have an accredited massage therapist program. Massage services are very reasonable: $30 for 1 hour, $40 for 1.5 hours, and $50 for 2 hours. They use the excellent Dermatologica line for their massage treatments, which is an added bonus. So you'll be glowing from sugar and salt rubs in addition to being all relaxed.

SOAKING & **SAUNAS**

Common Ground Wellness Center
5010 NE 33rd Ave.
(503) 238-1065
www.cgwc.org

Sometimes you just need to soak away your troubles. In addition to the natural hot springs detailed in the Escaping the City chapter, this can be accomplished at Common Ground Wellness Center, which offers as part of its menu of services chaste opportunities for hot-tubbing. This facility has soaking tubs and saunas; it is clothing-optional, but the atmosphere is designed to be nonsexual. They also have men-only hours, women-only hours, and transgender/gay-only hours, so everyone can relax without worrying. You can get an annual membership, and then your cost is only $7 for half an hour, but if you don't want to commit to that much wellness, you can pay $10. Best of all, on your birthday, you can have a 1-hour soak or sauna for free!

APARTMENTS & ACCOMMODATIONS

"Home is the place where when you have to go there, they have to take you in."

—ROBERT FROST

Portland is not the cheapest place in the country in which to buy or rent a house or apartment. For a variety of reasons, the housing costs here are on the higher end—even with falling real estate values. And houses and apartments in the core of the city—which are closer to transportation hubs and make it easier to bike or walk—are more expensive than those in the suburbs. That said, you will be able to find a great place in the city to live if you are patient and a little systematic.

Like most places, in Portland, Craigslist (www.portland.craigslist.org) is the go-to source for finding apartments and shared houses—and likewise, if you are seeking to reduce your housing costs by having a roommate, then this is the most common place to advertise. You should also check out the weekly paper *Willamette Week*; they will also have ads seeking roommates or alerting you to cheap but pretty vintage apartments or summer sublets. But if you are looking for even more discounted rent, try the programs below.

FREE **RENTAL** SERVICES

Housing Connections
www.housingconnections.org

Housing Connections is a free service that helps people find places to live. It was designed for low- and moderate-income people, but this free service can really be used by anyone. It covers housing in Multnomah, Clackamas, Washington, and Clark Counties, and its database contains more than 52,000 units of privately owned and publically subsidized housing.

The site is user friendly—it was built with advice from stakeholders, including property managers, housing agencies, and renters themselves. About 3,500 people search each week. You simply type in the area where you want to live, your price range, and the number of bedrooms you're looking for, and it pops up with a list of possibilities. You can further refine your search by filtering for pets, accessibility, smoking status, whether Section 8 vouchers are accepted, etc. It lets you know what schools are nearby, as well as whether it's near employers and TriMet. You can even view maps and photos so you can see whether you like the vibe of a particular place. Finally—it's not only used by renters. You can also find opportunities to buy houses as well.

Housing Connections has many community partners, including the housing authorities of Multnomah, Washington, and Clackamas Counties.

CHEAP **SLEEP**

Some people are looking for a cheap place to live—but some people are just looking for a place to rest their heads. Portland has two great hostels that are small communities in their own right, clean and friendly and cozy.

Portland Hawthorne Hostel
3031 SE Hawthorne Blvd.
(503) 236-3380
www.portlandhostel.org

The Catch: *If you are going to cancel, be sure you do this 24 hours in advance, or 48 hours if you've reserved a private room, or you will be charged for the first night. Also, Hostelling International has an annual membership fee of $28 for adults ages 18 to 54 and $18 for adults older than 55; the rates below are for members. Nonmembers will incur a $3 surcharge. You can buy a membership at the hostel. There's also a 12.5 percent lodging tax.*

The Southeast Portland hostel is on fun Hawthorne Boulevard in Southeast Portland, near the great shopping district, but also an easy walk to other attractions, such as food cart pods and popular music venues, with access to major bus routes as well.

If you sleep in the dorm, it will range from $20 to $24 per night, depending on the season. If you are traveling with children, they must be 7 or older to stay in the dorm rooms, but they will only cost you $10. If you are opting for a private room, the cost is $48 to $55 per night for singles and couples. Each additional person is $10 (children 6 and under stay for free in the private rooms). If you are biking through Portland, you can get a $5 per night discount. But they mean really riding your bike through Portland—not putting it on the train or on the back of the Hummer.

Portland Hostel, Northwest
425 NW 18th Ave.
(503) 241-2783
www.nwportlandhostel.com

This friendly hostel is in beautiful, Victorian Northwest Portland. It's within walking distance of much of what you would want to see, and it's close enough that you could walk from the train station, if you weren't carrying anything terribly large or heavy and you had some time to spare. (It's also close to the MAX line that takes you to the airport.)

The hostel is open all day, and they will give you lots of free stuff, including bread, maps, and wireless access, among others. Rates are $20 to $25, depending on the season, with children 14 and under half that. See the Portland Hawthorne Hostel listing for more details about membership and pricing.

HOUSE-SITTING

House-sitting can be a fantastic way to stay or reside cheaply in Portland, especially if you like pets. Many homeowners turn to house sitters not only to keep their houses occupied during an extended stay somewhere else but also because they have dogs, cats, birds, fish, chickens, or other pets that need care. In exchange for keeping the place running, you get the benefit of staying rent-free in a fully furnished house. You can also turn to Craigslist, but for targeted house-sitting opportunities, you can also try **House Carers** (www.housecarers.com). They provide an international matching service for those who need house sitters and those who would like to house sit, with helpful advice about drawing up agreements, liability, and other components of a successful venture. House-sitting may not be entirely free—you might have, for example, storage costs for your belongings, and it's common for house-sitters on extended stays to pay for utilities. Even with these costs, however, it's economical.

Exploring Portland

WALKING TOURS:
A CENTS OF PLACE

*"After a day's walk everything
has twice its usual value."*

—G.M. TREVELYAN

If you have a good rain jacket, Portland is a walker's paradise. Not only is the scale of the city walkable, but also it has more varied terrain than almost any urban area. You can walk through civilized plazas and squares or through acres and acres of quiet fields and forests and still stay within city limits. You can walk with groups and guides or you can explore on your own. In addition to the walks and tours collected here, you should also check out Metro's publication *Walk There*, which features 50 walks in historic Metro neighborhoods and wild areas. You can buy the book online or in stores—or you can download the 50 treks for free. Go to www.oregonmetro.gov and click on the "Sustainable Living" tab to find this resource. Another great source for walking events and information is **Portland Walking,** the blog of Laura Foster (http://portlandwalking.blogspot.com). She has written several books on walking in Portland (including *Walk There*). She often leads tours for groups, and then writes about them on her blog. You can use this free resource for reconnaissance before you try your own hike.

NATURE **WALKS**

Audubon Society Guided Walks
5151 NW Cornell Rd.
(503) 292-9453, (503) 292-6855
http://audubonportland.org

The Catch: Field trips are free, but they ask that if you attend, you try to carpool; also, they want you to wear binoculars as a sort of identifier.

The Audubon Society of Portland has a lush nature preserve in the northwest part of the city, which you can visit (for free!). But their free Birding Field Trips take you all across the natural areas in and around Portland, including Ankeny & Baskett Slough National Wildlife Refuge, the Gresham-Fairview Trail, the Sandy River delta, the Columbia River Gorge, the Ridgefield National Wildlife Refuge, Powell Butte, and Oaks Bottom. These field trips are led by volunteers, and from them you can learn all kinds of amazing things about the birds who live with us—as well as explore these beautiful areas in an organized fashion. The details of the individual trips are listed in the Events section of their website. Occasionally, they will want you to pre-register but most of the time you can just show up. (You can find other interesting but not free events on their website as well.)

Metro Park Tours
www.oregonmetro.gov

Portland is within a tri-county area that has a unique regional government, Metro. Metro organizes transportation and land use planning, and it runs the zoo. But it also is responsible for much of the natural space and parkland in the area, and it works with the city governments and nongovernmental agencies that maintain other natural areas and parks. These parks have free tours and activities, often hosted by local volunteers or businesses. Metro thoughtfully keeps these listed on a calendar on their website so that you can find out about them—if you are interested in the regularly occurring free events below, check this website for specific dates, times, instructions, and directions. They also publish a newsletter, *Metro Greenscene*, that has all their fabulous events (you can subscribe to the print version, the e-mail version, or just follow on Facebook or Twitter). You have to hand it to the bird watchers: They are very enthusiastic about sharing what they know, so many of the tours are bird-themed. But there are other topics too.

Jenkins Estate Guided Tour
Visit the beautiful 68-acre Jenkins Estate in Beaverton for guided tours with a focus on birds and wildlife. The splendid English-style gardens of the estate, designed and planted in the early 20th century, contain unusual plants, romantic pathways, and formal gardens as well as natural areas. Tours, which are sponsored by staff and volunteers from the Backyard Bird Shop, are free but require registration.

Magness Tree Farm Tour
The World Forestry Center sponsors a free guided tour of Magness Tree Farm in Sherwood on Sun from 2 to 3:30 p.m. Walk through the rows of trees to learn not only about sustainable forestry but also how to recognize various tree species.

Smith and Bybee Wetlands Tour
Smith and Bybee Lakes lie just south of the confluence of the Willamette and Columbia Rivers, near Kelley Point. They are said to comprise the largest

wetland within city boundaries, at 2,000 acres, and are managed by Metro. Experts from the Backyard Bird Shop offer free wildlife-focused tours of this interesting natural area. Requires registration.

Tualatin National Wildlife Refuge Tour

The Tualatin National Wildlife Refuge is a verdant natural area within the floodplain of the Tualatin River, near Sherwood—it's a primary spawning site for steelhead and salmon. If you want to know what the Willamette Valley used to look like before it was covered with subdivisions, big box stores, and grass seed farms, this is the place to check out. The Backyard Bird Shop folks will take you on a guided tour so you can learn more about it. Register in advance.

Tryon Creek Tour

Tryon Creek is a beautiful little state park in Lake Oswego with a dedicated nonprofit committed to developing loyalty to the park by hosting many interesting free events and celebrations. One such event is the guided tour for song bird identification. Volunteers from the Audubon Society will take you through its peaceful forests and wetlands to help you learn the calls and songs from native species.

Wetlands 101

This fascinating Metro-sponsored tour is preceded by an introduction to the biology and ecology of wetlands and their historical importance. After that,

---

Ten Toe Express

The City of Portland wants you to enjoy your city and get some exercise, so they offer a series of guided walks on Thurs at 6 p.m. and on Sat at 9 a.m. from May through Sept. These fun events tour some of the most beautiful and interesting neighborhoods in Portland, such as Irvington, Hollywood, and Overlook, with local experts to provide background on the history, architecture, and other details. All routes are planned for easy TriMet access. To join a walk, meet at the spot designated on the website www.portlandonline.com/transportation (sometimes more easily found by downloading the brochure).

---

you tour wetlands projects in the Columbia Slough to see how they are being managed. The workshop and tour are free; registration is required. Not ideal for young children, but teens are welcome.

GUIDED **TOURS**

Hoyt Arboretum Guided Walks
4000 SW Fairview Blvd.
(503) 865-8733
www.hoytarboretum.org/plan-your-visit/tours-and-walks

Lovely Hoyt Arboretum is essentially part of Washington Park. With 232 acres of trees and 10 miles of trails, it feels more forest than arboretum, but let's not let definitions stand in the way of enjoyment. The arboretum staff host guided talks on Sat at 10 a.m. and noon throughout most of the year. (They take a break during the winter rains.) Tours are about 90 minutes and cost $3. Here you will learn some history and a lot of botany and plant identification, which is very useful knowledge in Portland. To find the talks, you meet at the visitor center, and you don't need to make reservations. Once you know your foliage, you can download self-guided tours from the website; they have maps for tours of varying lengths and conditions from 1 to 4 miles.

Portland Walking Tours
(503) 774-4522
www.portlandwalkingtours.com

This outfit produces some excellent on-foot tours that are very well loved— particularly the Epicurean Excursion, which takes you on a tasting tour of some of Portland's best food, both high-end and low-key. They also have fun historical tours of Portland's odd side (believe me, there is one), and even a tour devoted to our city's burgeoning chocolate industry. The tours last about 3 hours and for the most part avoid major hill climbing. They are wonderful, but they are not at all cheap—tours are about $20 for adults for the basic tours, up to $60 for the Epicurean Excursion. However, if you watch the coupon sites and alerts, you can find amazing deals, like the time we found a Groupon special for 90 percent off. This is your best bet for discounted tours.

FREE **SELF-GUIDED** NATURE **WALKS**

The problem with guided tours is that they are group activities—which, you know, are not for everyone. Indeed, exploring nature in a group can seem a little contradictory. If this is how you feel, you are in luck: Portland has more park trails in its city limits than any other, so you can just hike in peace. Below are some of our favorite walks and hikes in natural areas in the city. Hikes outside the city can be found in the Escaping the City chapter.

Mt. Tabor Park
SE 60th Avenue and Salmon Street
(503) 823-7529
www.portlandparks.org
http://library.oregonmetro.gov/files/mounttabor.pdf

Everyone should have a place to go for restoration, and this park is a good choice. Mt. Tabor Park has 196 acres of trails, woods, reservoirs, grassy fields, playgrounds, and sports courts. Its trails are very popular with hikers and runners, and a climb up to the top affords spectacular views of Mt. Hood to the east, the wooded West Hills, and sweeping south to the Willamette Valley. Metro has an excellent self-guided walk (link noted above) that points out the public art in the park along with its many natural features. It has an interesting raptor population, and sometimes during winter twilight you can hear owls hooting away.

Oaks Bottom Wildlife Refuge
Portland Parks & Recreation
(503) 823-6131
http://library.oregonmetro.gov/files/sellwood_tooaksbottom.pdf

Oaks Bottom is a wetland right in the middle of Portland along the Willamette. It is gradually being restored through careful attention from volunteers (including area schoolchildren). It is adjacent to beautiful Sellwood

Park, and a walk along the top of the ridge through the park and down into the preserve is a fine way to spend an afternoon.

Elk Rock Island
Willamette River, near SE 19th Avenue and Sparrow Street, Milwaukie
www.portlandparks.org

Elk Rock Island is a volcanic rock in the middle of the Willamette River that is accessible through careful fording during low water (that is, summer). The park was donated to the city as a nature preserve and has some fine wildlife, particularly herons, hawks, egrets, and kingfishers. The hiking trail is well marked—stay on it to avoid poison oak.

FREE SELF-GUIDED CITY WALKS

In addition to self-guided hikes of natural areas, there are also some fantastic and popular walks through the city.

Eastbank Esplanade and Tom McCall Park
The Willamette River is the central geographic feature of the city, and its banks have been developed into a handsome public throughway on both sides of the river. You can stroll from the Hawthorne Bridge to the Steel Bridge, cross the river, and loop around to your starting point and see every variation of humankind. This 2.6-mile loop offers a great cityscape view, especially as you walk down the Eastbank Esplanade and look west, where the river bends off into forever. It's very pretty at sunset. One thing to note is that the Eastbank Esplanade parallels the freeway for a bit, and it can be noisy.

4T Trail: Trail, Tram, Trolley, and Train
http://library.oregonmetro.gov/files/trailtramtrolleytrain.pdf

The Catch: You'll need to shell out $2.35 for the TriMet ticket, which is good for 2 hours and gives you access both to the MAX and the streetcar. Make sure the tram (www.portlandtram.org) is operating on the day you plan to hike; occasionally it's closed for maintenance and it runs on Sunday only between Memorial Day and Labor Day.

This 4-plus-mile urban hike begins at the Washington Park Zoo, takes you along the top of the west hills to the highest point in the city—Council Crest Park—then through Oregon Health & Science University to the Portland Aerial Tram, down to the South Waterfront, and connects you to the Portland Streetcar, which connects to the MAX. You start by either riding the MAX to the Washington Park station or parking near the Oregon Zoo; then crossing US 26 to the Marquam Trail, which you follow to Council Crest. One fun feature of this hike is that you can ride the Aerial Tram for free—there is no cost for riding downhill. (It's $4 for a ticket to ride back up). This trail gives you spectacular views of the Cascades when it's clear. From Council Crest and the Tram, you can even see Mt. Rainier if the day is fine. While the trail is well marked with 4T signs, it is a little tricky in places—be sure to use the free map. In some ways, this is the quintessential walking tour of Portland. It takes you through popular attractions, beautiful residential areas, and quiet, forested hills; along the river; and on the best parts of the public transportation network. There's even a great espresso counter in OHSU's Center for Health and Healing at the bottom of the tram; you can stop in for a latte before you board the streetcar.

Southwest Trails
http://swtrails.org

Southwest Portland has 7 formal trails designated by signs, and these trails have an advocacy group that provides free maps to the trails, as well as news about their upkeep and status. They also have monthly guided walks through the lovely Southwest Portland neighborhoods and trails. These walks are held on the second Saturday of the month. Participants meet at 9 a.m. at the west entrance to Wilson High School; they usually finish up by noon.

FREE **GALLERY** WALKS

First Thursday
www.firstthursdayportland.com

First Thursday is the sprawling monthly celebration of art in downtown Portland and the Pearl District held on the first Thursday of each month from 6 to 9 p.m. or so. Art galleries and museums will stay open late to showcase new work, invite people in, serve them wine, and hope they buy some art. Show openings are timed to coincide with this free event, which is very, very popular. It is a good way to spend some time when you are low on cash—the free wine is nice, but it's also festive and can be mood-enhancing. However, parking—especially in the Pearl District—can be horrifying. (We park downtown and take the streetcar—the event venues are in the "Fareless Square" free zone!) Also, the action is pretty much over by 9 p.m. You can't go late or you'll miss the whole thing.

First Friday
www.firstfridayguide.com

You probably didn't know there was a Central Eastside Arts District. But there is, and they have some cool galleries whose shows open on the first Friday of the month. There are also music events and other fun free things, and a number of excellent bars, restaurants, coffeehouses, shops, and other businesses also participate. The nice thing about First Friday, besides its being on a Friday, is that the Central Eastside Arts District is less chaotic, so you can cover more ground and see more art. And it's generally easier to park. The streetcar will be running through this area by fall of 2011, so that makes it even more convenient and cheap. As with First Thursday, the main happenings are from 6 to 9 p.m., after which everyone goes home to sleep it off.

Last Thursday on Alberta Street
Last Thursday was originally developed as a bit of a countercultural riposte to First Thursday. Over time, as the Alberta Street neighborhood evolved into hipness, the event has become rather raucous—an evening-long monthly party. This has prompted hand-wringing among neighbors and local officials

as they try to figure out how to get people to behave themselves. But if you go on the early side, say 6 p.m., you will be delighted with the performances, gallery openings, shops, and other celebratory events. Just be sure to leave before the crowds get to be oppressive.

Time-Based Art Festival
www.pica.org/tba

The Time-Based Art Festival, sponsored by the Portland Institute for Contemporary Art, celebrates the aesthetics of the moment through live art. It attracts artists from across the spectrum—recently, the Plastics, Lone Twin, Rufus Wainwright, and the Wooster Group were in attendance. This 10-day festival dedicated to contemporary art of all stripes has many performances, workshops, and lectures; most of these are not cheap—in fact, passes to the festival are a couple of hundred dollars—but some of them are free to the public by their very nature. For example, a couple of years ago, an orchestra of guitars in Pioneer Courthouse Square turned into an en-masse walk to the Hawthorne Bridge where everyone watched performance art constituting a flotilla on the Willamette. So the trick is to study the schedule and position yourself well to take advantage of the public parts of the festival. See www.pica.org/tba for updated event information.

Southeast Arts Walk
http://snackword.netfirms.com/seportlandartwalk.com

The Catch: Since you are visiting artists' studios, you may feel some pressure to purchase something. But you don't have to.

The Southeast Art Walk comprises more than 200 artists, who open their studios for the first weekend in March to thousands of people. This event is free. You download a map and plan a route—because it's unlikely that you'll be able to see all the artists—and then walk from studio to studio. You can see artists of every possible variety at work. This is a peaceful approach to showcasing art that has some advantages to both artist and guest.

GARDENS & FORESTS:
FREE RANGE

"Life is bristling with thorns, and I know no other remedy than to cultivate one's garden."

—VOLTAIRE

Portland gets its share of rain—though not as much as Seattle, we like to point out. Still, all the rain does give us our lovely green city, as well as our dewy and youthful appearance. And the rain eventually gives way to a long, warm growing period that has lots of daylight. This is good news, because it means it is easy to grow things, and grow them cheaply or for free. You can spend a lot of money at the nursery, it's true, but puttering in the garden is something you can do for very low cost. You can compost. You can forage. You can take advantage of Freecycle and help out your neighbors by taking their unwanted plants. You can take inspiration from the excellent public gardens in Portland. You can grow food or you can just grow pretty plants that make you happy. In a life full of uncertainty, engaging with your garden puts pretty much everything into perspective.

FREE **GARDENS**

Crystal Springs Rhododendron Garden
Southeast 28th Avenue
(1 block north of Woodstock Boulevard)
(503) 823-3640
www.portlandparks.org

The Catch: A $3 admission applies during peak blooming period, from the first of March through Labor Day, if you go on any day other than Tues or Wed.

April and May are rhododendron time in Oregon, bringing hopeful signs of color after months of gray. Even when it is chilly and wet in May—which it can be—the jeweled brilliance adorning the rhododendrons, azaleas, and other native shrubs remind us that soon we will be able to remove our long johns. Crystal Springs Rhododendron Garden, set along a spring-fed lake in Southeast Portland, was initially developed as a test garden, which explains why there are more than 2,500 cultivated plants. While the spring is prime viewing for flowering shrubs, autumn is equally attractive in another way: the Japanese maples and sourwood trees give us one last brilliant blast of color before everything settles down for the winter. As noted above, adult admission is $3 from Mar 1 through Labor Day, so plan your visit for Tues or Wed. "Adult" refers to anyone older than 12. The park is open from dawn to dusk.

International Rose Test Garden

400 SW Kingston in Washington Park
(503) 823-3636
www.portlandparks.org

Portland's nickname (the one besides Stumptown) is the City of Roses. Every June, during the last part of the rainy, rainy spring, we celebrate the Rose Festival, with a Rose Parade, a Rose Queen, and a Rose Carnival. Our basketball team plays in an arena called the Rose Garden. We love roses, and have since 1888, when Georgiana Burton Pittock, who was the wife of the Oregonian publisher, held the first rose exhibition in her backyard. The International Rose Test Garden was established in 1917 (though not formally dedicated until 1927, if dates are important to you) on a gorgeous site in the west hills of Portland, above downtown, within Washington Park. It is a very, very popular tourist destination, not only because of the roses but also because you can see the city skyline, the Willamette River, and the Cascades, including Mt. Rainier on a good day. The garden comprises 5 acres and 8,000 plants, with more than 600 varieties of roses. Peak bloom time is June, usually, but flowers continue all through the summer and into the fall.

The Rose Garden has numerous gardens within its boundaries—for example, the charming Shakespeare Garden. This Elizabethan-style garden features the flowers, trees, herbs, and fruit found in Shakespeare's plays. Over time, roses named after Shakespearean characters have also been added. There is also a handsome sundial, as well as a memorial to William Shakespeare that was dedicated on his 382nd birthday (April 23, 1946).

Tours are available (free!) from June 1 through Sept 21. These are held on Tues at 11:30 a.m. and 1 p.m. and on Thurs, Sat, and Sun at 1 p.m. Tours begin at the Rose Garden Store, 850 SW Rose Garden Way (www.rosegardenstore.org).

Leach Botanical Garden

6704 SE 122nd Ave.
(503) 823-9503
www.leachgarden.org

In 1931, Lilla and John Leach bought some property along Johnson Creek in Southeast Portland from Jacob Johnson, who operated a profitable sawmill and for whom Johnson Creek is named. They then set about developing the property into a romantic house and garden, filling it with more than 1,500 varieties of native plants—ferns, wildflowers, shrubs, and bulbs. But the Leaches were no ordinary gardening couple: They were trained scientists and amateur botanists who went plant-hunting throughout the state. Eventually, they were responsible for discovering 11 new species of Northwest plants. In particular, the talented Lilla brought 5 new species to the attention of scientists, including *Kalmiopsis leachiana*, a rare, beautiful flowering shrub in the Kalmiopsis wilderness of southern Oregon.

The Leaches bequeathed their 14-acre estate to the City of Portland, and we are lucky to have this lovely synergy of art and nature to explore. John Leach, who was a successful pharmacist, was also president of the Oregon Arts & Crafts Society and a masterly metalworker, and his work is displayed throughout the estate. Lilla's artistic eye for plants is the main attraction, and her work is evident in the artfully composed natural gardens that make up the estate. Over the years, new features have been added that reflect her spirit, including rock gardens, bog gardens, and the beckoning pathways that meander along. It's one of the few remaining places in the eastern part of the city that allows you to imagine what the Willamette Valley looked like before freeways and strip malls. The garden is open Sun from 1 until 4 p.m. and Tues through Sat from 9 a.m. until 4 p.m.

SOMETIMES **FREE** GARDENS

Japanese Garden
611 SW Kingston Ave.
(503) 223-1321
(503) 223-9233 (for tours)
www.japanesegarden.com
www.japanesegarden.com/free

Portland's Japanese Garden is one of the most authentic outside of Japan and was designed by noted landscape designer Takuma Tono. This lovely and serene garden is composed of 5 distinct spaces: the Flat Garden, the Strolling Pond Garden, a Tea Garden with a ceremonial tea house, the Natural Garden, and the Sand and Stone Garden. Like others of its kind, the plants are only part of the show: It's the totality of the texture, surface, light, sound, and color, and how these variables play with one another and change with the season that make this a remarkable experience. Even in the rain, the garden is beautiful. It is very popular with tourists, so it's not only Portland natives who think this way.

The gardens are open every day except on Thanksgiving, Christmas Day, and New Year's Day, and guided tours are available—once you pay for admission, which is not cheap. Regular prices are $9.50 for adults, $7.75 for seniors and college students, $6.75 for students ages 6 to 17, and free if you happen to be younger than 5. However, there are deals: Local coupon books such as the Chinook Book and the Entertainment Book often have 2-for-1 deals, and college students and seniors pay only $5 admission on Thursday. But the best deal is their annual free day in November, when they don't charge admission. Guides are there to answer questions.

Lan Su Portland Classical Chinese Garden
NW 3rd Avenue and Everett Street
(503) 228-8131
www.portlandchinesegarden.org

One of the most inspirational gardens around is the Lan Su Portland Classical Chinese Garden. This is a stunning city garden, built in traditional Chinese style, that feels far larger than the block it inhabits. In the center is an 8,000-square-foot lake, surrounded by courtyards, walkways, and interior spaces. Gardens in the classical style have discrete spaces designed for contemplation, and within each space are beautiful tableaux of stones, trees, flowers, and other plants. Some plants are chosen for the sound they make when the raindrops fall on their broad leaves, while others are chosen for their symmetry or their fragrance. The contrasting textures are a major feature, as are the stunning rock arrangements, some of them imported from our sister city, Suzhou. One striking detail are the stones sculpted by rushing water in the streams near Suzhou—stones that were placed in the stream beforehand to be sculpted for 60 years. That's some long-term investment in art.

The garden is open daily, from 10 a.m. to 5 p.m. Nov through Mar, and from 9 a.m. to 6 p.m. Apr through Oct. Docent-led tours are offered regularly, and I highly recommend these: They elucidate details that you never would have noticed on your own. Normal prices are not cheap: $8.50 adults; $7.50 seniors older than 62; $6.50 student, including college students with ID. If you are younger than 5, you get in for free. But, as with the Japanese Garden, there are discount tickets in the Chinook Book and in similar venues. Better yet, at the beginning of January, the garden offers a week of free admission days to celebrate its birthday.

GARDENING **RESOURCES**

Master Gardeners
www.metromastergardeners.org

The Master Gardeners arm of the Oregon State University Extension Service works closely with the regional government, Metro, delivering a popular educational program in natural gardening. This low-resource style of gardening uses the natural properties of plants and their wise planting to give a bountiful harvest while avoiding pesticides and other chemicals. The program has an impressive array of free classes, demonstration gardens, and tours, as well as online videos and other resources. The Master Gardeners also produce a monthly e-mail newsletter that is exceptionally useful for information such as recognizing and dealing with common pests and weeds, in addition to notices about events and other pertinent information.

Portland Parks & Recreation Community Garden Program

The Catch: The wait list for garden plots can be several years or even longer.

Portland Parks & Recreation maintains 35 community garden sites across the city. Or rather, individuals and families maintain these coveted sites, growing produce and flowers that their yards at home cannot accommodate. This program does far more than just provide individual plots: It maintains a city fruit program to promote growing of berries and tree fruits; it organizes a surplus produce exchange so that those with too much produce can give it to needy people; it offers classes, workshops, and other resources; and so on. There are some annual costs for the plots, which can cost about $80 per year for a full plot or as little as $20 per year for a smaller raised bed, but depending on what you grow, this investment could be a true bargain. Financial assistance is possible, as well. As a community garden plot renter, you also must agree to follow certain rules about planting, clean-up, pests, and other civic-minded behavior.

Growing Gardens
www.growing-gardens.org/index.php

Growing Gardens is a local nonprofit that helps low-income people find space for, create, and maintain gardens to help with food security and improved nutrition. They actually help people build and install their gardens, they provide seeds and starts, and they have a mentoring program that lasts for 3 years to help people build skills. And they also offer sliding-scale classes that anyone can attend, even if you are not a member of the program. So if you want to learn how to join the multitude of urban chicken farmers (in Portland, you can have 3 hens), you can learn the basics of chicken keeping for as little as $5.

FORAGING

When I say "foraging," I emphatically do not mean "dumpster diving." Rather, I mean partaking of the unseen abundance all around us. I have friends who have a trained eye for abandoned fruit trees on city lots. I have other friends who will stop in the middle of a country bike ride, pull some things that look like weeds, and come home to make the most delicious pesto. I have other friends who know where all the wild blackberries grow and keep their families stocked with jam. One way to get cheap food is just to go out and collect it. This very old-fashioned approach to eating is seeing a renaissance in Portland and beyond.

Wild Food Adventures
www.wildfoodadventures.com

If you plan to try local harvesting, you should get some training in what is available, what is legal—and what is safe. You need to be careful about lead paint in yards with old houses, pollutants from nearby highways, and the toxic wastelands along railroad tracks. You also want to learn to distinguish the edible from the inedible, the benign from the poisonous. Wild Food Adventures is a resource providing classes, workshops, field trips, and exhaustive materials on these very topics. John Kallas, who heads Wild Food Adventures, is one of the nation's leading authorities on this topic.

First Ways
http://firstways.com

You might think that one danger of foraging is that we will run out of food if we all eat this way. I can assure you there is no danger of this happening. Rebecca Lerner demonstrates this with her widely publicized weeklong experiment in eating only foods that she had foraged, some of them rather sensational (e.g., ant eggs). Nevertheless, there are many delicious and useful plants out there, and her insights and classes in foraging will show you how to find them. She won't make you eat ant eggs, but she will teach you how to identify sorrels, wild mustards, and other edible and medicinal plants in the Portland urban environment.

Urban Edibles
www.urbanedibles.org; www.urbanedibles.org/search

Urban Edibles is an online resource that connects foragers with things they might want to eat, and they have an incredibly useful annotated map of where blackberries, pears, plums, chestnuts, fennel, wild garlic, and other plants and fruit can be found. Better yet, the notes state the status of the site—whether it is public and therefore available, whether ownership is uncertain, or whether the owner of the site has actually made it available to anyone who wants to harvest. This is so helpful for property owners, for example, who are too busy to process their own fruit but who hate to see it go to waste.

Foraging for Seafood

The Oregon Coast has a remarkably productive fishery—even in these challenging times. And because Oregon's beaches belong to the citizens, you can participate in that fishery. Butter clams, razor clams, mussels, scallops, crab: All of these are available to anyone with a pail, a shovel, a dandelion weeder, and some gloves, almost for free. You can combine a delightful outing to the coast with the delightful feeling of bringing home dinner without spending anything except the gas money.

Oregon's broad sandy beaches are great for clams, which should be harvested during low tides, while the large basalt formations that are prominent on the central coast and southwards are ideal for mussels. A few sites are off-limits, such as the marine "gardens" at Cape Kiwanda and Yachats, but these are typically well marked. One of the best resources is the Oregon Department of Fish and Wildlife. Their website has advice about where to go, how to go about harvesting, a weekly recreation report to keep you up to date, links to online license purchase, and even the tide tables: www.dfw.state.or.us/resources/fishing.

Foraging in the National Forests of Oregon
www.naturenw.org/forest-products.htm

National forests belong to all of us—not just timber and mining companies—and for this reason you get to find things in them and bring them home. Okay, maybe it's not that simple, but you can, with some restrictions, harvest many things from national forests. You can find large rocks for your garden, native plants, and Christmas trees, as well as mushrooms, berries, wildflowers, nuts, and firewood. It's legal to take these as long as you observe certain limits about quantities and locations, you are educated about not removing rare or protected specimens, and you have any necessary permits.

You will need a shellfish or fishing license: this will cost you $7 per year if you live in Oregon. If you're visiting, the cost is $11.50 for a 3-day license or $20.50 for an annual license. There are also some limits about what you can catch—for example, mussel harvest is limited to 72 per person per day. To make sure there's enough for everyone, you should limit what you take to what you can eat, as well as being mindful of the ecosystem from which you are harvesting. Tread lightly.

Before you go, you'll want to check to see if the harvest is open. Sometimes the Oregon Department of Agriculture shuts down the shellfish harvest because of red tide and other toxic and dangerous bacteria. Check their website at www.oregon.gov/ODA/FSD/shellfish_status.shtml and be sure to call the shellfish safety hotline for the real-time updates—it is updated faster than the web pages are: (503) 986-4728 or (800) 448-2474.

While it's not foraging, if you are so inclined, you can also drive west to Astoria, Oregon, or Ilwaco, Washington, which lie on either side of the mouth of the Columbia. There you can find really superb, fresh tuna that you can take home and can yourself for much, much cheaper than you can buy it commercially.

Mushroom Identification Class
Oxbow Park
www.oregonmetro.gov

The Catch: This class costs $10, and there's a separate fee of $5 to enter the park.

It's a good idea, if you are harvesting wild mushrooms, to make sure you know the death cap from the porcini. Metro offers a class every fall in identifying Oregon's mushrooms. This fills up quickly, so look for it in the spring and don't delay registering. And even if you have to pay for the class and the parking, at least you will be alive to enjoy the mushrooms.

MUSEUMS, PUBLIC ART & LIBRARIES:
FREE ACCESS

*"Art is the only way to run away
without leaving home."*

—TWYLA THARP

Some people collect things; some people take the extra step and turn their collections into a "museum." Portland has long been the home of odd, sometimes short-lived museums, such as Velveteria, which was dedicated to the world's most garish paintings on velvet, or the 24-Hour Church of Elvis, which was both a museum and performance art. While we wait for the next iteration to emerge, we can amuse ourselves at the more traditional venues such as the Portland Art Museum and the Multnomah County Library. All of these institutions support the literary and visual arts, as well as documenting our history and experience. Some of them are free always, while others are free occasionally, and still others are not free but can be cheap. Be sure also to check out the Child's Play chapter, which has even more museums and attractions not listed here. You can find a list of library branches in Appendix C.

FREE

Mike's Movie Memorabilia Collection
Movie Madness
4320 SE Belmont St.
(503) 234-4363
www.moviemadnessvideo.com

Movie Madness is a video store with a vast collection especially noted for its classic, independent, and foreign films and cult favorites; if they don't have it, the film has not been released to video, CD, or DVD. This is impressive enough in its own right, but they also have an interesting collection of movie memorabilia, such as one of Julie Andrews's dresses from *The Sound of Music* and the knife from *Psycho*. Open every day. You can also arrange for tours.

Multnomah County Library Central Branch
801 SW 10th Ave.
(503) 988-5123
www.multcolib.org

Portland loves, loves, loves its parks and libraries. We vote to increase our own taxes to pay for them—and in turn they do things like give us free access to books, DVDs, CDs, and even downloadable free music! Really! There are 19 branches in the Multnomah County Library system, serving neighborhoods across the city. The Central Branch is the crown jewel—it's a beautiful space with tall ceilings, majestic staircases, cozy nooks, and even a coffee bar. (It is in Portland, after all.) There are several major collections, such as the Henry Failing Art and Music Library, which has an important array of sheet music, as well as works on the history of painting, photography, and handicrafts. Among the most popular of the collections are the Meyer Memorial Trust libraries for science and business, while the John Wilson Room offers rare books and artifacts, such as the *Nuremburg Chronicle* (dating from 1493). The Central Library—as well as all the libraries—has many interesting events, classes, and exhibits, as well as an efficient lending system that allows you to borrow books from any branch. You can pick them up at a designated branch or have them sent to your house (there is a small fee for that last service). The Central Branch of the library is open every day: Mon through Sat, from 10 a.m. to 6 p.m., except on Tues and Wed, when it's open until 8 p.m.; Sun, the library is open from noon until 5 p.m.

Portland Police Museum
1111 SW 2nd Ave.
(503) 823–0019
www.portlandpolicemuseum.com

The Catch: Admission is free, but you need to call ahead—and bring photo ID.

This odd little museum shows the paraphernalia associated with the policing life: uniforms and badges as well as various weapons, handcuffs, and even the first traffic signal in Portland. There's a working jail cell as well. They also have a good collection of historical photos. Hours are Tues through Fri, 10 a.m. to 3 p.m.

Stark's Vacuum Museum
107 NE Grand Ave.
(503) 232-4101
www.starks.com

Household maintenance aficionados will appreciate this funny little museum dedicated to the vacuum. They have hundreds of vacuums in the total collection, and some of them lead you to wonder what they were thinking when

Fort Vancouver National Site

Fort Vancouver was originally built by the British not only as a fur-trading center, but also as an attempt to solidify Britain's claim to the entire Northwest Territory. Fort Vancouver became an American outpost in 1846 when a treaty between the United States and Britain established the 49th parallel as Canada's southern border. Now restored and administered by the National Park Service, the **Fort Vancouver National Historic Site** (1501 E. Evergreen Blvd.; 360-696-7655, ext. 10; www.nps.gov/fova) offers a look at frontier life through a range of restored buildings, exhibits and displays, and re-creations.

Adjacent to Fort Vancouver National Historic Site sits **Vancouver Barracks,** the first military post in the Oregon Territory. From this base, Americans explored Alaska, fought the Indian Wars, provided security to settlers, and developed an early network of roads, dams, and locks. From May 1849 to the present, Vancouver Barracks has been an active military post. To the north of the Fort Vancouver National Historic Site and just across a vast green is **Officers Row,** an immaculately restored and rare collection of 21 Victorian-era homes built between 1850 and 1906 by the federal government. The houses were the residences for the military officers and other government officials and their families assigned to Fort Vancouver. This is the only entire Officers Row preserved in the nation, though such housing was once common. In particular, the **Marshall House,** where Nobel Prize–winning General George C. Marshall lived, is restored to impressive effect.

This site is open from 9 a.m. to 4 p.m. daily during winter and 9 a.m. to 5 p.m. during summer. It's very cheap! Adults are $3; children 15 and younger are free. You can also pay $5 for the family.

You might also be interested in the **Pearson Air Museum,** also on the Fort Vancouver site (www.fortvan.org/pages/pearson-air-museum). This aviation museum showcases the Golden Age of Aviation in the 1920s and '30s. Pearson has been in operation since 1911, making it the oldest airport in the US. The museum includes a theater and computer flight simulators, but the real focus is the civil aviation developments from the 1920s to the 1940s. The museum has a separate entrance fee of $7, $5 for children.

they invented that. You will appreciate bagless technology and HEPA filters like never before. Hours are Mon through Fri 8 a.m. to 7 p.m., Sat 9 a.m. to 5 p.m., and Sun from 11 a.m. to 5 p.m.

Vietnam Veterans Memorial
4033 SW Canyon Rd.

Okay, so it's not Maya Lin, but nevertheless, Oregon's memorial to its Vietnam veterans is a beautiful and fitting tribute to the 57,000 men and women who served in the war and the 800 who are thought to have died. It's sited on 11 acres of land in the southwest corner of Hoyt Arboretum, above the World Forestry Center. Each Memorial Day, an honor guard of ROTC cadets from the University of Portland stands a silent 24-hour guard at the memorial. The ceremony and vigil ends with all the names of the dead being read aloud, to show they are not forgotten, and with the haunting sounds of "Taps" echoing through the trees and hills.

Vista House at Crown Point
40700 E. Columbia River Historic Hwy.
www.vistahouse.com

Vista House is a monument to Oregon pioneers and to the completion of the Columbia River Highway from Portland to Hood River in 1916. The view from Vista House, which is 733 feet above the Columbia River, is one of the state's most popular, dramatic, and beautiful sights. It can be reached by taking the Historic Columbia River Highway (Hwy. 30) off I–84 at Corbett (exit 22), 15 miles east of Portland.

Crown Point, where Vista House is sited, has been named as a National Natural Landmark, and Vista House is listed on the National Register of Historic Places. Here you will find breathtaking views of the Columbia River, the Cascades, and the Columbia Gorge, and it is a favorite location for romantic proposals, wedding photos, sunset watching, and overall landscape appreciation. It is particularly lovely at sunset, when the river in the west glows fiery orange, while in the east it blends into the cliffs and hills, settling into lavender twilight. Our family likes to come here to celebrate the summer solstice, but it's beautiful year-round. You should be aware of the wind, however, which can be fierce in the winter. Vista House is open spring through fall from 9 a.m. to 6 p.m. daily, and on winter weekends from 10 a.m. to 4 p.m., weather permitting; you will find a gift shop and espresso bar as well.

Wells Fargo History Museum

1300 SW 5th Ave.
(503) 886-1102
www.wellsfargohistory.com

Featured in the lobby of the Wells Fargo building is a small museum dedicated to matters financial and fiduciary. There is an impressive restored stagecoach, as well as displays on the history of banking, the settlement of the west, and Portland itself.

SOMETIMES **FREE**

Oregon History Museum

1200 SW Park Ave.
(503) 222-1741
www.ohs.org

The Oregon History Museum is dedicated to detailing and preserving the history of the state, beginning with the indigenous tribes and continuing through today. It's always interesting to view contemporary events through the lens of history, and many exhibits are designed to illuminate the present as much as they are to cast light on the past. The History Museum owns some prime real estate downtown, and for this reason—and because they have pictures of everyone and everything—they are a large force in the city. The museum has a free day every April—check their website for this annual event. On the third Saturday of the month, you can get 2 children in for free with every paid adult ticket.

Portland Art Museum

1219 SW Park Ave.
(503) 226-2811
www.portlandartmuseum.org

The Portland Art Museum is housed in a graceful building designed by Pietro Belluschi and is thought to be the oldest museum in the Pacific Northwest. It has expanded aggressively in the past few years, acquiring new space and new collections, including, for example, the personal collection of art critic Clement Greenburg and an impressive collection of Northwest and Native American art. It has a robust film department (the Northwest Film Center; see the Film chapter), as well as a beautiful sculpture garden and a cafe. The museum is free on the fourth Friday each month from 5 p.m. to 8 p.m., and kids under 18 are always free. Also see the Child's Play chapter.

CHEAP

Architectural Heritage Center
701 SE Grand Ave.
(503) 231-7264
www.visitahc.org

If there's one thing Portland likes to do, it's recycle old houses. This center, near Rejuvenation (see the Shopping chapter), is dedicated to making sure we recycle in an aesthetically and historically accurate way. They also hold workshops and tours and offer resources for people who want to restore their houses. The center rotates displays of different artifacts (e.g., historical doorknobs!), featured painters, and historical exhibits. Hours are Wed through Sat from 10 a.m. to 4:30 p.m. Admission is $3.

Museum of Contemporary Craft
724 NW Davis St.
(503) 223-2654
www.museumofcontemporarycraft.org

The Museum of Contemporary Craft offers an homage to the historical traditions of the Arts and Crafts movement, but does so with a contemporary eye. It features art and design from artists whose media include ceramics, glass, wood, metal, and fiber. We love that this gorgeous museum, which is affiliated with the Pacific Northwest College of Art, is in the old Daisy Kingdom building, which was a vast fabric and crafting store. It's free on the first Thursday of the month (during the First Thursday celebration); otherwise, it's $3 or $2 for students. Very cheap! You should pay more. Hours are Tues through Sat 11 a.m. to 6 p.m. (until 8 p.m. on First Thursday).

Oregon Jewish Museum

1953 NW Kearney St.
(503) 226-3600
www.ojm.org

The Oregon Jewish Museum has the singular responsibility of being the only institution in the Pacific Northwest bearing witness to Jewish history and culture. This peaceful museum also contains an archive of oral history, as well as temporary and permanent exhibits. It is not free but it is cheap—$6 for adults and free for anyone 12 and under.

Oregon Maritime Museum

On the waterfront at the foot of Southwest Pine Street between the Morrison and Burnside Bridges
(503) 224-7724
www.oregonmaritimemuseum.org

The Oregon Maritime Museum is appropriately set in a stern-wheeler tug, and if you love ships, this is the museum for you. It covers Portland's historic shipbuilding industry as well as paintings, old instruments, and other interesting artifacts. Even though we're 100 miles inland, Portland has had an outsized sea-going presence, and this museum documents this. The museum's hours are 11 a.m. to 4 p.m. Wed through Sat, and Sun from noon to 4 p.m. This museum will set you back $5 unless you are under 6 or in the military, in which case it is indeed free.

Oregon Museum of Science and Industry (OMSI)

1945 SW Water Ave.
(503) 797-4000
www.omsi.edu

The Catch: Parking is not free—it costs $2 per vehicle. The Omnimax, planetarium, and USS Blueback all incur separate charges as well.

OMSI is a large and popular science museum—one of the largest in the nation—that has many hands-on, interactive exhibits. Some of these are permanent, such as a fascinating one on human development, while others are visiting exhibits such as *Bodyworlds*. There's also a planetarium and an Omnimax theater, as well as the last diesel-powered submarine, the USS *Blueback*. OMSI is very popular on rainy winter weekends, and you can see why.

To see OMSI as cheaply as possible, visit on the first Sunday of each month, when admission is $2. Children 2 and under are free.

Oregon Nikkei Legacy Center
121 NW 2nd Ave.
(503) 224-1458
www.oregonnikkei.org

The Oregon Nikkei Legacy Center tells the story of the 110,000 Japanese Americans who were interned in camps throughout the west during World War II through its temporary exhibits and permanent collections. Hours are Tues through Sat from 11 a.m. to 3 p.m. Admission is $3 (suggested). Also be sure to check out the nearby Japanese American Historical Plaza in Waterfront Park. Broken, cut, and shattered stones represent the lives disrupted by this event.

The Oregon Zoo
4001 SW Canyon Rd.
(503) 226-1561
www.oregonzoo.org

The Catch: Beware of separate charges for train rides, other rides, and parking.

The Oregon Zoo is not as cheap as it once was, but it is still pretty great— one of the best in the nation, with dozens of exhibits in carefully constructed and realistic habitat. In fact, the zoo is noted for its attention to animal habitat and animal fertility. In addition to cute animals, the zoo is noted for being the sole surviving railway post office, with its own cancellation mark. You can mail your letters from there and see if anyone notices. Be sure also to check out the Salvador Dalí painting and other treasures in the Lilah Callen Holden Elephant Museum in the Elephant House. The Oregon Zoo is open every day except Christmas Day, from 8 a.m. to 6 p.m. in the spring and summer, and from 9 a.m. to 4 p.m. in the winter. To see the zoo as cheaply as possible, you should take the MAX; the ticket is worth $1.50 off the price of zoo entry. Regular adult admission is almost $10, so visit on the second Tuesday of each month, when tickets are $4.

Pittock Mansion
3229 NW Pittock Dr.
(503) 823-3623
www.pittockmansion.org

The Catch: Entry costs $6 unless you are younger than 6 or you are a volunteer.

Pittock Mansion is the former residence of one of Portland's most prominent citizens, Henry Pittock. He was the original publisher of the *Oregonian*, still the state's paper of record. The turn-of-the-20th-century chateau has 22 rooms and more than 16,000 square feet, and you can tour the house and grounds to see how the 1 percent lived. The house is maintained by the City of Portland, as are the spectacular grounds, though these are shared by the Audubon Society. The Pittock Mansion is open for public viewing 7 days a week from 11 a.m. to 4 p.m., except in July and Aug, when it opens at 10. It's beautiful every time of year, but especially at Christmas, when local musicians make the whole experience very festive. Volunteering is one way to visit Pittock Mansion often for free.

Rice Northwest Museum of Rocks & Minerals
26385 NW Groveland Dr.
(503) 647-2418
www.ricemuseumnw.org

The Rice family were rockhounds, and they started showing off their remarkable collection of agates in 1938 and then added many more mineral, rock, and other natural "found objects" for you to marvel at. It's a favorite field trip destination. Hours are Wed to Sun from 1 to 5 p.m.; tickets are in the $5 to $7 range, depending on your status.

World Forestry Center
4033 SW Canyon Rd.
(503) 228-1367
www.worldforestry.org

This industry-inspired museum is dedicated to the giant trees that once lined the area and to those that felled them. Interactive exhibits offer information opportunities for hands-on lessons focusing on the forests of the Pacific Northwest and beyond. There are also adventure rides—for example, a white-water "rafting" trip and a 45-foot lift up into the tree canopy (these carry small extra charges beyond the price of admission). You will also find shops, rotating exhibits, and an annual event showcasing the talents of woodworkers and their amazing carving talents. To see it cheaply, visit on Wednesday, when admission is discounted to $2 per person. Parking costs $2 per vehicle.

ART RESOURCES

Multnomah Arts Center (MAC)
7688 Southwest Capitol Hwy.
(503) 823-2787
www.portlandonline.com/parks

The Multnomah Arts Center occupies a pretty building that once was a junior high school, and true to its roots, it is a mecca for anyone looking to learn a new arts-related skill. MAC offers design and art classes for all ages. You will find art classes for everyone, from toddlers dabbling with mom and dad to preteens learning cartooning, to serious graphic artists using the right side of their brains. There are burgeoning theater, music, and dance departments as well as classroom and hall rentals. It is also home to the Basketry Guild and Portland Handweavers Guild. Visit the website to download a catalog.

Portland Institute for Contemporary Art
224 NW 13th Ave.
(503) 242-1419
www.pica.org

PICA is an advocacy group and gallery that is highly active in the community; they stage the Time-Based Art festival every year, a gala event that unfolds over weeks, modeled after the Edinburgh Festival. PICA provides residence and other forms of sustenance to artists, as well as education, exhibition, and performance programs. There is a resource room with hundreds of exhibition catalogs, periodicals, DVDs, and books on contemporary art, as well as an archive of all past PICA productions. It's open to the public Mon through Fri from 10 a.m. to 5 p.m.

ESCAPING THE CITY:
FREE AT LAST

"The real voyage of discovery consists not in seeing new landscapes, but in having new eyes."

—MARCEL PROUST

As much as we adore Portland, one of the principal reasons we live here is to get out of it—that is, to enjoy the beautiful mountains, desert, and beaches but still have a job that pays for our treks out of town. We've already covered cheap recreation, but sometimes the spirit moves you to go farther afield.

CAMPING **IN** OREGON

www.oregonstateparks.org
www.oregonstateparks.wordpress.com

It is possible to camp in Oregon for very little money at all, especially if you are, say, hiking the Pacific Coast Trail and just bivouacking wherever you can clear some rocks off the pine needles. Yet some people find such commitment daunting. Some people just want to find somewhere cheap to stay at the beach with their children or their friends.

In Oregon state parks, you can camp in a yurt or a cabin or a fire lookout for less than $50 per night—and sleep in a bed, sit at a table, play cards with an electric lamp, and keep warm by a heater. Of course, you can also sit outside by a fire and look at the stars. But you don't have to, since the parks listed below have another property that makes them civilized: They are very near and sometimes in towns—towns with things like espresso machines and bookstores and brew pubs—or even vacation rentals and hotels for the in-laws, where they can be even more civilized than you, though at much greater cost.

Yurt and cabin sites often have room for tents as well; there is, however, a limit to how many cars you can park at a given site, and extra vehicles cost $5 each. If you or a guest are planning to stay just for the day, you'll need a state park pass ($5 per day or $30 for the year; during April, you can get an annual pass for the low, low price of $25—or a 2-year pass for $50. Buy now and save!).

If you rent a yurt or another facility, you should be aware of a couple of things. During peak periods such as the warm summer months, you have to be a little flexible about timing your stay—or else plan ahead 9 months, the outer limit of the reservation system. You can't cook in the yurt, so you either have to eat out or picnic. The yurt sites do have outdoor picnic tables and fire pits for cooking and sitting around, but you can't bring your camp stove inside the yurt. Many yurts also have covered porch areas, however. You will pay $5 for extra vehicles and $4 per bundle of firewood. As of this writing, you can't let Fido (or any other pets) into state park yurts or cabins, though they are pilot testing dedicating some of these facilities to campers with pets for an extra charge. Our dog sleeps in the car, and she's fine. Finally, you are camping, so the bathroom facilities, including hot showers, are a short walk from the camping sites, not actually in the yurts. We can always dream.

The sites below are near towns and are managed by the Oregon State parks program, but the U.S. Forest Service rental program is another fabulous, if not quite as civilized, approach to camping. They rent out structures on Forest Service land, such as old fire lookout cabins on the tops of mountains or ranger stations in lush forests. These run from about $40 to $60 per night and typically sleep 4 to 6 people. Some of these spots have room for extra tents outside. They are mostly very remote, and you'll need to pack in water and climb the towers multiple times to bring up your gear—and ski in for several hours if you are renting in winter. But watching twilight fall from a lookout with vistas of 3 states might be worth the hassle.

OREGON COAST

Fort Stevens
Off US 101, 10 miles west of Astoria
www.oregonstateparks.org/park_179.php

A favorite incredibly civilized place to camp is Fort Stevens, near the Oregon-Washington border. It has 2 main features that make it civilized: Its proximity to the wonderful town of Astoria, at the mouth of the Columbia River, and its internal properties. Externally, its civilized features include the fact that it is a few minutes' drive from at least 3 museums, including the interesting Columbia River Maritime Museum and the historic Flavel House; excellent regional food at the unbelievably good Bowpicker Fish & Chips, which serves beer-battered albacore tuna chips and steak fries (cheap!), as well as the sumptuous Bridgewater Bistro (not cheap, but you can afford it because you are camping!); and bracing ales at the Fort George Brewery and Public House. In addition, you can hear live music and poetry readings, visit the

Astoria Column, reminisce about your favorite scenes from *Goonies*, which was set and shot here, and generally enjoy this proudly blue-collar/hipster working town before you cuddle into your down sleeping bags and listen to the hum of the space heater back at the yurt. Even better, you can have civilization right at the yurt's door: What could be more civilized than a museum devoted to war? Fort Stevens was an actual military fort from the Civil War era through World War II, and a museum documenting its history is on site, as well as interesting information and exhibits about the gruesome "Graveyard of the Pacific," which illuminates all the carnage begot by ships trying to cross the Columbia River bar. Transitions are dangerous.

Yurts are $41 per night—there are also deluxe cabins, but these are not nearly as cheap.

Nehalem Bay State Park
Off US 101, 3 miles south of Manzanita
www.oregonstateparks.org/park_201.php

You can learn everything you need to know about our family by our attitude toward lodging: It's either a 5-star hotel or camping. If we can't have a luxury suite somewhere, we would rather have the autonomy and economy of a campsite. That's why we head to Nehalem Bay State Park, just outside Manzanita, on the northern Oregon coast. Manzanita is a beautiful town with a long, sandy beach, and a lovely state park along its southern border. It is possibly the most civilized place on earth to camp. This is because you can stay at a yurt, with space heaters and beds and electricity, have a glass of wine and look at the stars, get up in the morning and instead of going to the trouble of fussing with the fire or the camp stove, you can drive 2 minutes to one of the best coffee shops on the coast, Manzanita News & Espresso. There, you can eat a gingerbread scone and have a double Americano while you read the *New York Times* or *Film Quarterly*. Manzanita has other charms as well—spas, bookstores, excellent restaurants, a natural foods market and a great community grocery store, a wine bar, high-end clothing, doughnuts, bike rentals, a beautiful beach to walk on . . . in short, everything you need for a civilized get-away for $36 per night, plus firewood.

THE BEND AREA

Tumalo State Park
5 miles west of Bend, on the Deschutes River

Tumalo State Park is nestled along the lovely, rushing Deschutes River among fragrant sage, juniper, and pine trees in the high desert of central Oregon and very near to Bend. Bend is on the dry side of the Cascades; it is warm and clean in the way that things are when they are baked in the sun. This exceptionally attractive resort town is a magnet for golfers, skiers, and other fans of every kind of outdoor recreation. Bend has grown fast over the past decade, transforming from a sleepy resort backwater to the juicy destination town it is today. But it's expensive to stay at Sunriver or Black Butte. A cheap alternative is, therefore, the beautiful, beautiful yurts at Tumalo. Frankly, this is one place I would stay in a tent—even cheaper!—as long as I could have the Aerobed.

Why it's civilized: Bend is right there!! Great coffee! Brew pubs! The High Desert Museum! Lava trails! Sage and juniper, ponderosa pines! Yurts are $35 to $43 per night.

DAY **HIKES,** SWIMMING **HOLES** & WATERFALLS

In the Walking Tours chapter, we covered hikes within the actual city limits of Portland. But there are also dozens of hikes within an hour's or so drive of Portland. Here are 7 that we never get tired of and that are not too far away—nobody else seems to get tired of them either, so if you need more peace and quiet, many books and websites are devoted to the hiking in Oregon. Be sure to check them out.

Coyote Wall

The Catch: You'll need to pay a toll ($1.50—or more precisely, 75 cents per axle) to cross the Hood River Bridge, both ways. If you are too cheap for that, which would be a pity, then you can take the longer way, SR 14 on the Washington side.

Coyote Wall is a beautiful basalt outcropping across the Columbia River from Hood River (on the Washington side of the river). It's at the eastern edge of the "rain shadow" that blankets the Cascades, where the Columbia bends toward the northeast, offering vistas of the green gorge as it begins to fade into the warm, golden dryness of the high desert. This is a 6-mile round-trip hike that winds through open oak forest and grassy meadows before you reach the top of the wall and the unbelievable views of the Columbia Gorge and Mt. Hood. It's also noted for the dozens of different kinds of wildflowers blooming in the spring, as well as for the unique rock formations along the way. The wall itself stands above oak and evergreens and scrub brush, and the river far below, jutting upward like a castle fortification. From its top, you can see down the Gorge in both glorious directions.

To get there: Take I-84 to Hood River, cross the bridge, and continue east about 3 miles to Bingen. Park in one of the gravel parking lots at Courtney Road. Walk up Courtney Road to the gate. Climb over or under the gate, and continue on the road east on Hwy. 8. You will shortly reach an old cattle chute that marks the junction with the Coyote Canyon Trail. Turn left and join the trail here.

Things to watch out for, besides the sheer drops in some places, are poison oak and lots of ticks. In fact, every time I see someone's Flickr stream of hikers lying down in the meadow at the top of the wall, I start itching. Also, bikers love this trail, which was really built for them, so be mindful of who else is out there when you're hiking, and keep Fido on the leash.

Dog Mountain
WA 14, milepost 53
Columbia River Gorge

The Catch: If you take the Bridge of the Gods, you'll pay a $1 toll each way.

Dog Mountain is a popular hike about 12 miles east of the Bridge of the Gods, near Skamania, on the Washington side of the Columbia River. Like Coyote Wall, its popularity is largely due to its amazing views of the Gorge, its wildflowers, and its proximity to Portland. You'll work in the first half mile as the trail climbs about 700 feet. At this point, you will reach a junction offering 2 approaches to the top of the mountain at 2,984 feet: the east trail, which is longer but not as strenuous, or the west trail, which is more hard work but is shorter. We prefer the east trail because its views are better.

Dogs are welcome on Dog Mountain, but keep them leashed. Watch out for rattlesnakes, black bear, and poison oak. To get there, take I-84 east to exit 44, at Cascade Locks. Take the toll bridge north to WA 14, turn right, and continue east on WA 14 until you reach the trailhead between milepost 53 and 54, on the north side of the highway. Incidentally, the Bridge of the Gods is the official Columbia River crossing for those hiking the Pacific Crest Trail.

Eagle Creek/Punchbowl Falls
Eagle Creek Park

The Catch: Requires a forest parking permit ($5 for the day or $30 for an annual pass).

To get to Eagle Creek Park, take exit 41 off I-84 (also the exit for Bonneville Dam). Turn right off the exit and stay right along the road until it ends in the parking lot. It can get crowded on summer weekends, so your best bet is to get there early.

This 4-mile round-trip hike is one of the most beautiful in the Gorge, winding along swift-moving Eagle Creek. The trail begins and ends at creek level, but as you travel south and gain elevation, it takes you high above the creek—very high in some places. This trail was evidently built by Italian engineers about 100 years ago, to coincide with the inauguration of the Columbia Gorge Highway. If you have ever driven in Italy, this will make perfect sense to you, for the trail at times has been blasted out of the sides of cliffs, with an iron cable attached to the cliff wall for the heights-phobic on one side, and a very sheer high drop into the creek on the other side. My hands get sweaty just thinking about it. These bits of the trail are not long, but they demand caution, so this is not the best trail for small children or unruly dogs. (We did hike with our daughters here when they were babies in backpacks, though.) Continue along the trail until you get to the 1.5-mile point, at which time you can take a short detour to observe Metlako Falls. Back on the trail, about 0.3 miles later, you'll see the sign for Lower Punchbowl Falls. This trail takes you to the creek, with broad rocks on which you can picnic or sunbathe, views of Punchbowl Falls, and access to the punchbowl itself, which is the goal on a hot, sunny day. You can also stay on the main trail, continue for about a quarter mile, and look at the falls from above, at the Punchbowl Falls overlook.

You can continue on the Eagle Creek Trail—many hikers take the trail all the way up to Tunnel Falls, turning the outing into a 12-mile hike round trip. Others follow the trail until it eventually connects with the Pacific Crest Trail and extend the day hike into a 3-day backpacking adventure. (Eagle Creek is a popular detour off the Pacific Crest Trail, so it works both ways.)

Elowha Falls
I-84, Ainsworth Park exit from Portland (exit 35)

In the deep heat of July, one of our favorite swimming holes is Elowha Falls. This pretty, easy hike leads you up, and then down, a 1.4-mile trail to a verdant waterfall that spills into a large bowl. It's not too deep, and it's very cold, and it's safe for children as long as you're keeping a watchful eye on them. No diving! You'll break your neck! Of course, you can go there other times of the year as well—the falls are misty and cool, but there are many sunny rocks to sit on for an autumn picnic. The creek spills below, and the rocks are suitable for clambering about. I mentioned that we like to visit on hot days—so does half of Portland, so it can get crowded.

To get to the trail, turn left from exit 35, then make a quick right onto the frontage road. Take this road about 2 miles, to John B. Yeon Park. You'll see the signs for the trailhead.

Multnomah Falls and Larch Mountain
Off I-84 at exit 31
(503) 695-2372
www.multnomahfallslodge.com

Portland natives can become inured to the idea of Multnomah Falls, ostensibly the second-highest waterfall in the US. (It's easy to claim something is second-best. Who would check?) But they should not: No matter how many times you see it, it remains inscrutable and alluring. You can visit for free and let the mist from the falls refresh you and then just turn around and go home, or you can use this gorgeous site as the beginning of a number of hiking adventures, since the trailhead leads to an array of adventures of varying length and difficulty.

One popular hike is the easy Multnomah Falls loop, which is about 3 miles. From the visitors' center, take the paved path to the bridge beneath the falls. Linger awhile, and then continue to the top of the falls, about 1 mile. There is a beautiful viewpoint there as well. When you've had your fill of the view, you can then do a couple of things. You can take the trail along the ridge west of the falls to Upper Wahkeenah Falls, and continue until you reach the junction for the Perdition Trail. Stay right along this trail for a little more than a mile. You will traverse several stone staircases, and just past the longest one, you'll reach the Wahkeenah Trail. Take this, staying to the right and passing Upper Wahkeenah Falls. The trail turns to pavement again about half a mile before Wahkeenah Falls. Stay on the path above and parallel to the Columbia Gorge Scenic Highway for about another half mile, until you reach the Multnomah Falls parking lot. This hike is about 3 miles. (You can also do it the other way around, starting from the west end of the Multnomah Falls parking area; that way you end your hike with the most exciting view.)

But if you crave a longer outing, you can take the Multnomah Falls trail all the way to Larch Mountain, which is a round-trip hike of about 14 miles that takes almost 8 hours—and is worth every minute. At the top, on a clear day, you can see north all the way to Mt. Rainier, as well as Mt. St. Helens, Mt. Adams, Mt. Hood, and Mt. Jefferson, rising above the beautiful foothills of the Cascades. Waterfalls, mountain peaks—this is as close to perfect as a day hike can get.

Turn upcreek from the Upper Multnomah Falls viewpoint, continuing along the Larch Mountain trail into the verdant forest. The trail follows the creek for 3 miles, passing all 3 Dutchman Falls (lower, middle, and upper), as well as through the Dutchman Tunnel. At this point, the trail reaches Weisendanger Falls, then continues upward to Ecola Falls, and keeps along the creek (if the water is high, there's a well-marked alternate route). Keep following the signs—you'll eventually cross a road and the east and west forks of Multnomah Creek. At this point, the climb becomes very steep. Larch Mountain is more than 4,000 feet, and you'll be rapidly gaining elevation. When you reach the top, make the effort to take the 0.25-mile Sherrod Trail, a paved walk to the lookout, to be rewarded for your hard work and to rest before you bang up your knees on the way back down.

Silver Falls State Park

Oregon Highway 214, 26 miles east of Salem
(800) 551-6949 (information)
www.oregonstateparks.org/park_211.php

The Catch: Requires a $5 day-use pass.

Silver Falls State Park is a mysterious sylvan oasis tucked into the foothills of the Cascades. Here you will find numerous trails winding around, behind, and between giant firs and cascading waterfalls. (A detailed map of all the trails is available on the park's website, listed above). The Trail of 10 Falls (really there are more than 10) will take you along most of them. The Canyon Trail, which encompasses part of the Trail of 10 Falls, will take you along the banks of the north and south forks of Silver Creek, where you will be able to view a variety of different falls, from the impressive South Falls (177 feet) to the gentle Drake Falls (27 feet). To preserve its pristine nature, there are no shelters, picnic tables, or restrooms along the Silver Creek Canyon Trail, but the park itself offers plenty of facilities, including a lovely swimming area further up the creek.

Silver Star Mountain

www.wta.org/go-hiking/hikes/silver-star-mountain
www.portlandhikersfieldguide.org/wiki/Silver_Star_via_Grouse_Vista_Hike

Beautiful Silver Star Mountain is on the Washington side of the Columbia River, just east of Vancouver. From there, you can see sweeping views of the central Cascades—nearby Mt. Hood, Mt. St. Helens, and Mt. Adams, but also Mt. Rainier and Mt. Jefferson. For this reason, and for the gorgeous late spring and early summer wildflowers, it's a popular hike. There are several trails; from Portland, the most efficient is probably the Grouse Creek Vista trail (#180F). This 6-mile round-trip trail covers the south approach, and it's about an hour's drive from Portland. Of course, this is also the most difficult of the trails, with the highest elevation gain, but it has the most interesting terrain. You'll want good boots and poles. Note that the Silver Star trail, #180, is probably the most popular, and it is a more family-friendly hike but requires more time in the car over some very rough road. You might not want to subject the Zipcar Prius to that kind of treatment. It could get expensive! See the above links for more information on the different approaches. Depending on which trail you use, you may need a Northwest Forest Pass.

To reach the Grouse Creek Vista Trail, take I-205 until exit 27, toward Camas, and merge onto WA 14, turning left at Salmon Falls Road. Continue on this road, turning left after 1.5 miles to stay on Salmon Falls, until Washougal River Road. Turn right and stay on Washougal River until Hughes Road. Turn left at Hughes, continue up Hughes, and at the county line, turn left at Skamania Mine Road. Turn left at FR 1200, which leads to the trailhead.

HOT **SPRINGS**

Oregon has several dozen natural hot springs that can be found in the foothills of the Cascades. Most of them are on public land, although one facility, Breitenbush (www.breitenbush.com) is privately owned. If you are not feeling cheap, you can enjoy this luscious retreat by the day or stay overnight; call for fees and reservations. But if you are cheap, you can visit hot springs for free. Note that many visitors to Oregon's hot springs regard clothing as optional. If you yourself are more comfortable in a swimsuit, be aware that your fellow hot-springers might be unconcealed, so to speak, and plan accordingly. Other tips: Leave glass, dogs, and soap at home.

Bagby Hot Springs
Off Highway 224, in the Mt. Hood National Forest, Clackamas County

The Catch: Requires a Northwest Forest Pass ($5 daily; $30 annual) to park in the area.

Bagby Hot Springs, on U.S. Forest Service land southeast of Portland, is the closest geothermal soaking pool area to the city, and it is understandably very popular—so much so that the Forest Service is contemplating putting the site under private management before it is loved to death. In the meantime, however, it's free to enjoy the warm water and soak in the cedar tubs. To get there, take I-205 to exit 12 to Highway 224. Stay on Highway 224, through the town of Estacada, all the way until it ends. You'll see the Ripplebrook Ranger Station; here, the highway becomes Forest Service Road 46. Remain on this road for about 3.5 miles until FR 63. Turn right; stay on this road until you reach FR 70, about 3.6 miles. Turn right again. The parking lot for the hot springs is approximately 6 miles past the intersection of FR 63 and FR 70, to your left. You'll then take a short hike, about 1.5 miles, to the springs.

Cougar/Terwilliger Hot Springs
East of Blue River, Oregon, Willamette National Forest, off Highway 126

The Catch: Requires a Northwest Forest Pass ($5 daily; $30 annual) to park in the area.

Terwilliger Hot Springs—or, as popularly known, Cougar Hot Springs— requires a day trip from Portland, since these natural pools are east of Eugene. Terwilliger Hot Springs comprise 5 pools that cascade down, one to the next. The highest pool is the hottest, so be mindful of the temperatures—it really is quite hot. To get there, drive south on I-5 until the freeway intersects with Highway 126, at the north end of Eugene. Head east, continuing on Highway 126 until you reach the exit for the Cougar Reservoir, which is FR 19, between mile markers 45 and 46. Take this road until you reach the dam, a little more than 3 miles, then turn right, which leads you west around the reservoir. Stay on this road for approximately 4.3 miles until you reach the trailhead to the hot springs.

ADDITIONAL RESOURCES

Living cheaply means being able to take advantage of bargains in real time—that is, in knowing where to look. The following resources help with this task.

CALENDARS, **EVENTS** & DISCOUNT **SHOPPING**

Around the Sun
http://aroundthesunblog.com

Around the Sun is a blog dedicated to finding cheap and free things to do in Portland. They send a handy weekly e-mail on Friday that summarizes the week's upcoming free events.

Portland Picks
www.portlandpicks.com

Portland Picks is an online guide and newsletter targeted to women interested in fashion, restaurants, style, and design. It is the best source of information for sample sales, discounted local designs, fitness deals, and fun events like wine tastings and store openings. While not everything they feature is cheap, they offer many coupons and other specials. Portland is not on the Daily Candy radar, so this is a fine alternative. You can subscribe to the newsletter and see it in time for the weekend.

Red Tricycle Portland
www.redtri.com/portland-events

Red Tricycle is a west-coast resource guide for families that covers free events as well as style and design, parenting issues, ideas for crafts, birthday parties, and pretty much the kinds of things you would find in any magazine for families. But they have a great weekly e-mail newsletter that covers events for families; you can sign up and filter for the city you live in as well as your areas of interest. Not all the events are free, but many are. Other cities covered by Red Tricycle include Seattle, San Francisco, Los Angeles, and San Diego—that's handy to know if you are planning to travel to one of these cities, since there are lots of ideas for free events and other fun things to do.

COUPONS & **DEALS**

In addition to the coupons mentioned in the Shopping chapter (Chinook Book and Frugal Living Northwest), and elsewhere in the book (Goldstar .com), the following online discounts are useful.

Fabulessly Frugal
http://fabulesslyfrugal.com/coupon-insert-lists/portland

This couponing site is a Pacific Northwest–focused resource for deals galore. They have exhaustive advice about couponing, including a binder-driven method for "clipless" couponing, in which you don't clip the coupon until your item is in the cart. This saves a lot of time organizing. The Portland insert list noted above does all the work of comparing coupons and deals for you and gives you a web page, Excel file, or PDF that you can print out and use for your shopping trips. This is an idea we can all get behind. Thanks, Fabulessly Frugal!

Groupon
www.groupon.com

Fabulous daily deals that guarantee the merchant a certain level of business and you a substantial level of discount. The coupons are valid when a predetermined number of people purchase the discount. Groupon is used by many Portland businesses for a variety of things, from restaurants to personal services to clothing to events—and even the food carts!

Living Social
www.livingsocial.com

Living Social is similar to Groupon—one deal per day—but without the minimums.

Restaurant.com
www.restaurant.com

In restaurant-crazy Portland, this coupon program is a great way to sample. You purchase a coupon—for, say, $10—that gives you a $25 gift certificate to participating restaurants. You can purchase different amounts (e.g., a $100 gift certificate for $40). Many good restaurants are in this program. Unless the tip is already included in your bill, be sure to tip on the amount that you would have paid on the total bill before discount, or your restaurant karma will be terrible.

Online Portland Attractions Pass
www.travelportland.com/deals/more-savings-1/portland-attractions-pass

If you have visitors from out of town (or if you are from out of town—or maybe taking a stay-cation), you can get passes that allow you to buy discounted admission to a number of area attractions. The pass is valid for 5 days (you choose the start date) and is good for 1 adult per pass. They are only available online. You may be asked for ID when you enter an attraction. Also, there may be service charges for tickets and some special exhibitions at the Portland Art Museum may require additional fees. Still interested? Then here are the details.

Big Pass: $53.55 (save $21.95)
This gives you entry into the following: Lan Su Chinese Garden, Oregon History Museum, Oregon Zoo, Pittock Mansion, Portland Art Museum, Portland Children's Museum, Portland Japanese Garden, World Forestry Center.

Washington Park Pass: $31.50 (save $12.50)
This pass includes the following: Japanese Garden, Pittock Mansion, Portland Children's Museum, Oregon Zoo, World Forestry Center.

Downtown Pass: $22.05 (save $9.45)
This pass buys entrance into the following: Lan Su Chinese Garden, Oregon History Museum, Portland Art Museum.

Garden Pass: $17.85 (save $8.15)
This pass covers the following: Lan Su Chinese Garden, Pittock Mansion, Portland Japanese Garden.

CHEAP **CLASSES**

Portland Community College Community Education
www.pcc.edu/community

Portland Community College is the largest organization of higher education in the state, and this highly regarded 2-year college is responsible for some of the best education experiences around. But in addition to their degree programs, they have an amazing variety of community education classes. These are organized into creative arts (drawing, ceramics, painting, writing, photography, etc.); home and garden (crafts, home improvement, sustainable living, wine appreciation, cooking); languages and culture (conversation classes, basic classes, languages for travelers, and so on); sports and fitness (yoga, dance, nutrition, sports); and work-life balance. This latter group is especially good for people who are trying to brush up their resumes or improve their Excel skills—you can take many of these classes online and receive a certificate.

Portland Parks & Recreation
www.portlandparks.org

Community centers at Portland Parks & Recreation (see Appendix B) also offer a staggering variety of really, really cheap classes, organized by target audience (preschool, youth, teen, adults, seniors). Summer swimming lessons are a rite of passage for kids in Portland, while their grandparents are in the pool doing water aerobics. But this is only the beginning—there are also classes in cartooning, ceramics, knitting, jewelry, sculpture, home improvement, cooking, languages, botany, golf, theater, dance, and on and on.

PARKS & RECREATION COMMUNITY CENTERS

A staple of any cheap lifestyle is utilizing the 13 extensive, clean, and handsome community centers operated by Portland Parks & Recreation. They hold classes in arts and crafts, languages, sciences, and other interesting things, as well as fitness, dance, swimming, and sports. You can rent rooms for parties and gatherings as well. To find out more information about these facilities, go to www.portlandparks.org.

Community Music Center
3350 SE Francis St.
(503) 823-3177

East Portland Community Center & Pool
740 SE 106th Ave.
(503) 823-3450

Fulton Park Community Center
68 SW Miles St.
(503) 823-3180

Hillside Community Center
653 NW Culpepper Ter.
(503) 823-3181

Laurelhurst Dance Studio
3756 SE Oak St.
(503) 823-4101

Matt Dishman Community Center & Pool
77 NE Knott St.
(503) 823-3673

Montavilla Community Center & Pool
8219 NE Glisan St.
(503) 823-4101

Mt. Scott Community Center & Pool
5530 SE 72nd Ave.
(503) 823-3183

Multnomah Arts Center
7688 SW Capitol Hwy.
(503) 823-2787

Peninsula Park Community Center & Pool
700 N. Rosa Parks Way
(503) 823-3620

Sellwood Community Center
1436 SE Spokane St.
(503) 823-3195

Southwest Community Center & Pool
6820 SW 45th Ave.
(503) 823-2840

University Park Community Center
9009 N. Foss Ave.
(503) 823-3631

St. Johns Community Center
8427 N. Central St.
(503) 823-3192

Woodstock Community Center
5905 SE 43rd Ave.
(503) 823-3633

INDOOR **SWIMMING** POOLS

Buckman Pool
320 SE 16th Ave.
(503) 823-3668

Columbia Pool
7701 N. Chautauqua Blvd.
(503) 823-3669

East Portland Community Center & Pool
740 SE 106th Ave.
(503) 823-3450

Matt Dishman Community Center & Pool
77 NE Knott St.
(503) 823-3673

Mt. Scott Community Center & Pool
5530 SE 72nd Ave.
(503) 823-3183

Southwest Community Center & Pool
6820 SW 45th Ave.
(503) 823-2840

OUTDOOR **SWIMMING** POOLS

Creston Pool
SE 44th Avenue and Powell
Boulevard
(503) 823-3672

Grant Pool
NE 33rd Avenue and US Grant Place
(503) 823-3674

**Montavilla Community Center
& Pool**
8219 NE Glisan St.
(503) 823-4101

**Peninsula Park Community
Center & Pool**
700 N. Rosa Parks Way
(503) 823-3620

Pier Pool
N. Seneca St. & St. Johns Ave.
(503) 823-3678

Sellwood Pool
7951 SE 7th Ave.
(503) 823-3679

Wilson Pool
1151 SW Vermont St.
(503) 823-3680

LIBRARY LOCATIONS

MULTNOMAH **COUNTY** LIBRARY

The Multnomah County Library system (www.multcolib.org) has a branch near you. More branch information can be found at their website.

Albina Library, 3605 NE 15th Ave., (503) 988-5362
Belmont Library, 1038 SE César E. Chávez Blvd. (SE 39th Ave.), (503) 988-5382
Capitol Hill Library, 10723 SW Capitol Hwy., (503) 988-5385
Central Library, 801 SW 10th Ave., (503) 988-5123
Fairview-Columbia Library, 1520 NE Village St., (503) 988-5655
Gregory Heights Library, 7921 NE Sandy Blvd., (503) 988-5386
Gresham Library, 385 NW Miller Ave., (503) 988-5387
Hillsdale Library, 1525 SW Sunset Blvd., (503) 988-5388
Holgate Library, 7905 SE Holgate Blvd., (503) 988-5389
Hollywood Library, 4040 NE Tillamook St., (503) 988-5391
Kenton Library, 8226 N. Denver Ave., (503) 988-5370
Midland Library, 805 SE 122nd Ave., (503) 988-5392
North Portland, 512 N. Killingsworth St., (503) 988-5394
Northwest Library, 2300 NW Thurman St., (503) 988-5560
Rockwood Library, 17917 SE Stark St., (503) 988-5396
Sellwood-Moreland Library, 860 SE 13th Ave., (503) 988-5398
St. Johns Library, 7510 N. Charleston Ave., (503) 988-5397
Troutdale Library, 2451 SW Cherry Park Rd., (503) 988-5355
Woodstock Library, 6008 SE 49th Ave., (503) 988-5399

WASHINGTON **COUNTY** LIBRARIES

www.wccls.org/libraries

Banks Library, 111 Market St., (503) 324-1382

Beaverton Library
www.beavertonlibrary.org
Main Branch, 12375 SW 5th St., (503) 644-2197
Murray Scholls, 11200 SW Murray Scholls Place, Ste. 102, (503) 644-2197

Cedar Mill Community Library
Bethany Branch, 15325 NW Central Dr., Ste. J-8, (503) 617-7323
Main Branch, 12505 NW Cornell Rd., (503) 644-0043

Cornelius Public Library, 1355 N. Barlow St., (503) 357-4093
Forest Grove City Library, 2114 Pacific Ave., (503) 992-3247
Garden Home Community Library, 7475 SW Oleson Rd., (503) 245-9932

Hillsboro Library
Main Branch, 2850 NE Brookwood Pkwy., (503) 615-6500
Shute Park Branch, 775 SE Tenth Ave., (503) 615-6500

North Plains Public Library, 31334 NW Commercial St., (503) 647-5051
Oregon College of Art & Craft, 8245 SW Barnes Rd., (503) 297-5544
Sherwood Public Library, 22560 SW Pine St., (503) 625-6688
Tigard Public Library, 13500 SW Hall Blvd., (503) 684-6537
Tualatin Public Library, 18878 SW Martinazzi Ave., (503) 691-3074
Tuality Health Resource Center, 334 SE 8th Ave., (503) 681-1702
West Slope Community Library, 3678 SW 78th Ave., (503) 292-6416

OTHER **USEFUL** LIBRARIES

Lake Oswego Public Library
706 4th St.
(503) 636-7628
www.ci.oswego.or.us/library

Oregon Health & Science Library
3181 SW Sam Jackson Park Rd.
(503) 494-3460
www.ohsu.edu/xd/education/library/index.cfm

Health and biomedical research information services.

INDEX

Academy Theater, 16

A.C. Gilbert Museum, 115

Aladdin Theater, 35

All Classical FM, 39

Alpenrose Dairy, 112

Amtrak, 100

Annie Bloom's Books, 50

Antoinette Hatfield Hall, 5

An Xuyen Bakery, 70

arcade games, 108

Architectural Heritage Center, 192

Arlene Schnitzer Concert Hall, 5

Around the Sun, 209

Artichoke Music, 35

Artists Repertory Theater, 3

art resources, 196

attractions, children's, 112

Audubon Society Guided
   Walks, 167

Aveda Institute Portland, 154

Baby and Me Outlet—Hillsboro, 123

Bagby Hot Springs, 207

Bagdad Theater, 22

Bailey's Taproom, 83

Ballroom Dance Company, The, 31

Bar Avignon, 59

barbers, 157

Barfly, 87

Barnes & Noble, 50, 110

Beau Monde, 155

beauty school drop-in, 154

beauty services, 154

Beaverton Civic Theatre, 7

beer festivals, 85

beer tastings, 83

Beezoo Exchange, 123

Bella Institute, 156

bella stella, 123

Belmont Station, 84

Bend area, camping, 201

Best Baguette, 71

Better Bargains Thrift Store, 124

Bhaktishop, The, 150

Bicycle Repair Collective, 99

Bicycle Transportation Alliance
   (BTA), 98

Biddy McGraw's Irish Pub, 35

Bike Portland, 98

bike repair, 99

biking, 96

biking resources, 97

Bishops Barbershops, 157

Biwa, 59

blogs, 209

Blue Monk, 36

Blue Monkey Theater Company, 11

Bodyvox, 28

brewery tours, 88

Broadmoor, 142

Broadway Books, 50

Broadway Rose New Stage Theatre, 4

Brody Theater, 7

Buckman Pool, 214

Buffalo Exchange, 120

Bunk Sandwiches, 71

Burgerville, 71

Burnside Skate Park, 109

calendars, 209
camping, 198
Canby Ferry, 107
car sharing, 93
Cartopia, 64
cart pods, 64
Cascade Brewing Barrel House, 84
Chamber Music Northwest, 43
Cheers to Belgian Beers, 85
children's activities, 103
Children's Place, 111
Children's Resale, 123
children's theater, 11
Chinook Book, 127
Chinook Book Deals, 14
Ciao Vito, 59
Cinema 21, 17
Cinemagic, 17
City Liquidators, 129
city walks, 172
classes, cheap, 212
Clinton Street Theater, 18
Clyde Common, 60
CoHo Theater, 8
Columbia Pool, 214
Columbia Sportswear Outlet, 130
"Comma," 47
Common Ground Wellness
    Center, 159
community centers, 213
Community Cycling Center, 99
Community Music Center, 41, 213
Compass Repertory Theatre, 8
concert series, 43
consignment stores, 124
Cork • A Bottle Shop, 79
Cosmic Monkey Comics, 51

Cougar/Terwilliger Hot
    Springs, 208
Country Cat, 72
couponing, 127
coupons, 210
Coyote Wall, 202
Craigslist, 118
Craigslist Rideshare, 101
Creston Pool, 215
cross-country skiing, 147
Crossroads Trading Co., 121
Crystal Ballroom, 36
Crystal Springs Rhododendron
    Garden, 177
C-Tran, 92

Daisies & Dinos Resale and
    Consignment, 123
dance instruction, 31
dance performances, 28
day hikes, 201
Detour Cafe, 72
discount shops, 129
Distillery Row, 88
Dive-in Movies, 25
Dog Mountain, 202
do-it-yourself supplies, 131
Do Jump!, 28
Doug Fir Lounge, The, 36
drinks, 79

Eagle Creek/Punchbowl Falls, 203
Eastbank Esplanade, 172
Eastmoreland, 142
Eastmoreland Garage Sale, 119
East Portland Community Center &
    Pool, 213, 214

East-West College of the Healing Arts, 158

Edgefield Power Station Theater, 22

Electric Castles Wunderland, 108

Elk Rock Island, 172

Elowha Falls, 204

E & R Wine Shop, 80

Eugenio's, 72

Every Day Wine, 80

Excalibur Comics, 51

Fabulessly Frugal, 210

fairs, 105

farms, 105

fashion, 120

Fertile Ground, 12

festivals, theater, 12

film, 16

film events, 26

Fir Point Farms, 106

First Friday, 174

First Thursday, 174

First Ways, 183

First Wednesdays, 47

fitness, 140

Flicks on the Bricks, 25

Flower Farmer, 106

food, 58

food carts, 64

Food Carts Portland, 66

food, cheap, 70

food, foraging for, 182

food, free samples, 68

foraging, 182

Foraging in the National Forests of Oregon, 184

Fort Stevens, 199

Fort Vancouver National Historic Site, 189

Foster and Dobbs, 80

4T Trail: Trail, Tram, Trolley, and Train, 172

Freecycle, 119

Free Geek, 131

free movies, 23

free theater, 7

Frugal Living Northwest, 127

Fuller's Restaurant, 73

Fulton Park Community Center, 213

Gabriel Park, 103

gallery walks, 174

gardening resources, 181

gardens, 177

gear, outdoor, 128, 145

Get Rich Slowly, 121

Glendoveer Golf Course, 142

Goldstar.com, 14

golf, 140

Good Food Here, 64

Goodwill, 124

Goodwill Outlet, 125

Grant Park, 104

Grant Pool, 215

Great Wine Buys, 80

Ground Kontrol Classic Arcade, 109

Groupon, 210

Growing Gardens, 182

Hair of the Dog Brewery and Tasting Room, 84

Hanna Andersson Outlet, 130

happy hours, 58

Ha VL, 73

health care, 135
health care, alternative, 136
health clinics, 135
Heron Lakes Golf Course, 142
Hillside Community Center, 213
Hippo Hardware and Trading
   Company, 131
Hollywood Theatre, 18
Holocene, 37
Hoot-N-Annie, 123
hostels, 163
hot springs, 207
hot tubs, 159
house-sitting, 164
House Spirits, 89
Housing Connections, 162
Hoyt Arboretum Guided
   Walks, 170
Huber's, 60

In Other Words, 51
Irving Park, 104, 149

Jackpot Records, 37
Jake's Famous Crawfish, 61
Jake's Grill, 61
Jamison Square, 104
Japanese Garden, 179
JAW, 12
Jefferson Dancers, 29
Jeff Morris Fire Museum, 112
Jenkins Estate Guided Tour, 168
J & M Cafe, 73
Justa Pasta, 73

Keller Auditorium, 5
Kennedy School Theater, 22

Kerr Repair Kiosk, 100
Kidd's Toy Museum, 113
KOi Fusion, 66
Korkage Wine Shop, 81
Kuts 4 Kids, 157

La Jarochita, 67
Lake Oswego Golf Course, 143
Lake Oswego Public Library, 218
Lakewood Center for the Arts, 4
Lan Su Portland Classical Chinese
   Garden, 180
Larch Mountain, 204
Last Thursday on Alberta Street, 174
Laurelhurst Dance Studio, 213
Laurelhurst Park, 104, 149
Laurelhurst Theater and Pub, 18
Laurelthirst Public House, 37
Leach Botanical Garden, 178
library locations, 216
Lincoln, 61
Liner & Elsen Wine Merchants, 81
Little Edie's Five and Dime, 122
Living Room Theaters, 19
Living Social, 211
Loggernaut, 53
Lounge Lizard, 126

Mactarnahan's Taproom, 85
Magness Tree Farm Tour, 168
Magpie, 122
Marshall House, 189
massage, 158
Master Gardeners, 181
Matt Dishman Community Center &
   Pool, 213, 214
MAX Red Line, 101

McCormick & Schmick's Seafood
    Restaurant, 61
McMenamins Theater-Pubs, 22
Metro Paint Store, 132
Metro Park Tours, 168
Metropolitan Youth Symphony, 39
Mike's Movie Memorabilia
    Collection, 187
Miracle Theater, 4
Mission Theater, 22
Mississippi Marketplace, 65
Mississippi Studios, 37
Modern Thrifter, 121
Monday Night Movies, 24
Montavilla Community Center &
    Pool, 213, 215
Moreland Theatre, 19
Mountain Writers, 48
Mount Scott Community Center, 108
movies, 16
Movies in the Park, 24
Mt. Hood Meadows, 144
Mt. Hood Skibowl, 145
Mt. Hood Snosport Swap, 145
Mt. Scott Community Center & Pool,
    213, 214
Mt. Tabor Fine Wines, 81
Mt. Tabor Park, 105, 149, 171
Multnomah Arts Center (MAC),
    196, 213
Multnomah County Health, 135
Multnomah County Health
    Department STD Clinic, 137
Multnomah County Library, 38, 48,
    110, 216
Multnomah County Library Central
    Branch, 187

Multnomah Falls, 204
Murder by the Book, 51
Museum of Contemporary Craft, 192
museums, cheap, 192
museums, children's, 112
museums, free, 187
museums, sometimes free, 191
Mushroom Identification
    Class, 185
music, classical, 39
music, community, 41
music festivals, 43
Musicfest Northwest (MFNW), 44
Music Millennium, 38
music news, 34
music venues, 35

National College of Naturopathic
    Medicine, 136
Nature of the Northwest
    Information Center, 140
nature walks, 167, 171
Nehalem Bay State Park, 200
New Seasons Market, 68
Next Adventure, 128
Nicholas, 74
99W Drive-In Theatre, 23
Nonconsumer Advocate, 120
Nong's Khao Man Gai, 67
Nordstrom Rack, 130
Northwest Children's Theater, 11
Northwest Film Center, 20
Nourishment, 67

Oaks Bottom Wildlife Refuge, 171
Officers Row, 189
Off the Griddle, 67

Old Portland Hardware, 132
Online Portland Attractions Pass, 211
open mics, 47, 55
Oregon Ballet Theatre, 29
Oregon Brewers Association, 83
Oregon Brewers Festival, 86
Oregon Children's Theater, 11
Oregon coast, camping, 199
Oregon Culinary Institute, 74
Oregon Health & Science
    Library, 218
Oregon History Museum, 191
Oregon Jewish Museum, 193
Oregon Maritime Museum, 193
Oregon Museum of Science and
    Industry (OMSI), 113, 193
Oregon Nikkei Legacy Center, 194
Oregon Repertory Singers, 39
Oregon School of Massage, 159
Oregon Symphony, 39
Oregon Zoo, The, 115, 194
outdoor recreation, 140
outlets, 129

parks, 103
Paul Mitchell—The School, 156
PBJ's Grilled, 67
Pearson Air Museum, 189
Peer-to-Peer Car Sharing, 94
Peninsula Park Community Center &
    Pool, 213, 215
Pho Nguyen, 75
Pho Van, 75
Pier Pool, 215
Pittock Mansion, 195
Pivot, 137
Pix Movie Night, 23

Planned Parenthood, 138
playgrounds, 103
Play It Again Sports, 129
Pok Pok, 75
Polaris Contemporary Dance
    Center, 30
Por Que No, 76
Portland Afoot, 95
Portland Art Museum, 191
Portland Arts & Lectures, 53
Portland Ballet, The, 30
Portland Beauty School, 156, 159
Portland Center for the Performing
    Arts, 5
Portland Center Stage, 5
Portland Chamber Orchestra, 40
Portland Children's Museum, 114
Portland City Grill, 61
Portland City Pools, 148
Portland Community College
    Community Education, 212
Portland Concert Co-op, 34
Portland Dancesport, 31
Portlander Cinema, 21
Portland Farmers' Market, 42,
    69, 105
Portland Hawthorne Hostel, 163
Portland Hostel, Northwest, 164
Portland Institute for Contemporary
    Art, 196
Portland International Beerfest, 86
Portland International Film
    Festival, 26
Portland Jazz Festival, 44
Portland Opera, 6
Portland Parks & Recreation, 108,
    141, 212

Portland Parks & Recreation
  community centers, 213
Portland Parks & Recreation
  Community Garden Program, 181
Portland Picks, 209
Portland Playhouse, 8
Portland Poetry Slam, 55
Portland Police Museum, 188
Portland Saturday Market, 42
Portland State University, 65
Portland Story Theater, 9
Portland Timbers, 151
Portland Trailblazers, The, 151
Portland Transport, 95
Portland Transportation Office, 97
Portland Walking Tours, 170
Portland Wine Merchants, 81
Portland Winter Hawks, 151
Portland Youth Philharmonic, 40
Potato Champion, 68
Powell's Books, 52, 111
Press Club, 38
Profile Theatre, 9
Pumpkin Patch, The, 107

Readers Theatre Repertory, 9
Reading Frenzy, 52
Reading Local: Portland, 49
readings, 47
real estate, 162
Rebuilding Center, The, 132
Red Light Clothing Exchange,
  The, 122
Red Tail Golf Course, 143
Red Tricycle Portland, 209
Rejuvenation, 133
rental services, 162

Rerun, 126
Restaurant.com, 211
Rice Northwest Museum of Rocks &
  Minerals, 195
River City Bicycle Outlet, 129
Rose City Golf Course, 143
Roseway Theater, 21
Rudy's Barbershop, 158

Safeway Classic Golf
  Tournament, 152
salons, 157
Sapphire Hotel, 76
saunas, 159
Savvy Plus, 123
SCRAP, 133
seafood, 184
Sellwood Community Center, 213
Sellwood Pool, 215
sexual health, 137
Shakespeare in the Park—Portland
  Actors Ensemble, 7
Sherman Clay Pianos, 41
Silver Falls State Park, 206
Silver Star Mountain, 206
skateboarding, 109
ski areas, 144
Smith and Bybee Wetlands
  Tour, 168
Sno-Park permit, 144
Sno-Park Ski Areas, 147
snowshoeing, 147
Southeast Arts Walk, 175
Southwest Community Center &
  Pool, 214
Southwest Trails, 173
Spints Alehouse, 62

sports, 140

sports, spectator, 151

Star E Rose, 49

Stark's Vacuum Museum, 188

St. Johns Community Center, 214

St. Johns Theater, 22

Stone Barn Brandyworks, 89

Storyteller Wine, 82

story times, 110

streetcars, 93

Stumptown Stages, 10

Summer at the Square, 43

Summer Free for All, 43

Summit Ski and Snow Play
    Area, 146

Sushi Ichiban, 77

Sweet Peas, 123

swimming, 148

swimming holes, 201

swimming pools, indoor, 214

swimming pools, outdoor, 215

Tanuki, 62

Tasty N Sons, 62

Teacup Lake, 147

Tears of Joy Theater, 12

tennis, 149

Ten Toe Express, 169

theater, 3

theater, cheap, 7

theater festivals, 12

theaters, alternative movie, 23

theaters, independent movie, 16

Third Rail Repertory Theatre, 10

Thirst Wine Bar & Bistro, 82

3D Center of Art and
    Photography, 113

3 Friends Mondays: Caffeinated
    Art, 49

thrift stores, 124

tickets, discount, 14

Timberline Lodge and Ski Area, 146

Time-Based Art Festival, 175

Time Bomb Vintage, 123

Tin House Writers Workshop, 53

Title Wave, 131

Tom McCall Park, 172

Toro Bravo, 77

tours, brewery, 88

tours, distillery, 88

tours, guided, 170

tours, walking, 167

Trader Joe's, 69

transportation, public, 91, 100

Trebol, 63

Trillium Lake Snowtrails, 148

TriMet, 91

Tryon Creek Tour, 169

Tualatin Hills Aquatic Center, 148

Tualatin National Wildlife Refuge
    Tour, 169

Tumalo State Park, 201

Twilight Repertory Theater, 10

University Park Community
    Center, 214

Urban Edibles, 183

Urban Farmer, 63

ushering, 3

Valley Cinema-Pub, 21

Value Village, 126

Vancouver Barracks, 189

Vespers at Trinity Cathedral, 42

Victory Bar, 63
Vietnam Veterans Memorial, 190
Village Merchants, 126
Vino, 82
Vinopolis, 83
Viscount Dance Studios, 32
Vista House at Crown Point, 190

walking, 95
walking tours, 167
Washington County Libraries, 217
Washington Park, 105
waterfalls, 201
Waterfront Blues Festival, 45
Wells Fargo History Museum, 191
Well Suited, 124
Wetlands 101, 169
Whiskey Soda Lounge, 75
White Bird Dance, 30
Whole Foods, 70
Widmer Brothers Brewing
    Company, 88

Wild Food Adventures, 183
William Temple House Thrift
    Store, 128
Wilson Pool, 215
wine tastings, 79
Woodstock Community Center, 214
Wordstock: A Book and Literary
    Festival, 54
World Forestry Center, 116, 195

yoga, 150
Yoga Shala, 150
Yoga Union, 150
youth and children's theater, 11

Zell's, 77
Zipcar, 94
ZoomCare Neighborhood Clinics, 135
Zwickelmania, 87